JAPANESE STREET SLANG

JAPANESE STREET SLANG

PETER CONSTANTINE

Boston • WEATHERHILL • London

WEATHERHILL
an imprint of Shambhala Publications, Inc.
Horticultural Hall
300 Massachusetts Avenue
Boston, Massachusetts 02115
www.shambhala.com

© 1992 by Peter Constantine
Cover illustration by Kasei Inoue

First edition, 1992
Eleventh printing, 2008

Printed in the United States of America
This edition is printed on acid-free paper that meets the
⊗ American National Standards Institute Z39.48 Standard.
Distributed in the United States by Random House, Inc.,
and in Canada by Random House of Canada Ltd

Library of Congress Cataloging in Publication Data

Constantine, Peter, 1963–
Japanese street slang / by Peter Constantine. — 1st ed.
p.   cm.
Romanized Japanese phrases with English translations.
ISBN 978-0-8348-0250-6
1. Japanese language—Slang.   I. Title
PL697.C66 1992
495.6'83421— dc20   92-4205
                                                          CIP

CONTENTS

Foreword vii

Introduction xi

Acknowledgments xxiii

Japanese Street Slang 3

References 175

Japanese Word List 177

Index 187

FOREWORD

One reason why I have gotten more pleasure and less exasperation from studying Japanese than from studying Chinese is that the dictionaries of Japanese are so much better: when I need information about the meaning, usage, and pronunciation of Japanese words, I can consult works that give me relatively easy access (easy, at least in relation to the obstacles that are posed by what is without doubt the world's screwiest writing system) to detailed and reliable information about the words. And when I use Japanese dictionaries, whether bilingual ones or monolingual dictionaries such as an educated Japanese would use as a reference work on his native language, I am usually rewarded with a kind of pleasure that I often experience in Japan or when dealing with mechanical or intellectual products that emanate from Japan: the joy of appreciating master craftsmanship and of feeling vicariously the pride that the craftsman takes in a job well done. Chinese chefs have often given me that type of pleasure (which enhances the purely sensory pleasure given by the products of their kitchens), but Chinese lexicographers have not.

However, despite the extraordinarily high standards that have been observed in Japanese lexicography, perhaps the highest standards that are maintained for dictionaries of any language, there are major gaps in the standard dictionaries of Japanese, and Peter Constantine's *Japanese Street Slang* fills many of these gaps. Japanese dictionary makers have given no more than sporadic coverage to the numerous words that are generally regarded as impolite or vulgar, and have thereby helped to foster the widely held misconception that Japanese is deficient in those important areas of vocabulary. *Japanese Street Slang* will leave no doubt in any reader's mind that Japanese is as rich as any European language in words that refer raunchily to all known forms of sexual activity, that refer contemptuously to mental, moral, anatomical, and physiological shortcomings of other persons, or that make light of conditions ranging from flatulence and bad breath to pregnancy and poverty.

Standard dictionaries likewise give little if any coverage to vocabulary that is the property of particular occupational groups, social milieus, and other segments of Japanese society rather than of the society as a whole. True, there is extensive coverage of the technical vocabularies of science, engineering, medicine, and biology, but those vocabularies are still conceived of as belonging to Japanese society as a whole, unlike the words that doctors use when talking informally with other doctors, or computer nerds when talking informally with other computer nerds, which do not make it into the dictionaries and remain in the mouths, ears, and minds of the members of those specific subcultures. *Japanese Street Slang* provides a wealth of information about the vocabularies of several subcultures that are far from the center of polite Japanese society: not only the worlds of prostitutes, gays and lesbians, drug users, and thieves, but also that of teenagers, whose vocabulary changes as rapidly as does that of their American counterparts and is also about as opaque to their elders. The difference between the vocabularies that are in the dictionaries and those that are not is like the difference between *vous* and *tu* in French: if you're not a dentist, you can use words like "incisor" and "premolar" to refer to teeth, but you'd better not ask your dentist to "check for caries upper left four, mesio-buccal," since only those who are entitled to say *tu* to the field of dentistry are entitled to use that kind of language. When the author of *Japanese Street Slang* tells his readers to be very careful about using the words that he introduces them to, his message isn't so much that you shouldn't say *fuck* to your Aunt Hilda as that you shouldn't say *tu* to subcultures that you're only entitled to say *vous* to, and it may be useful to think of his warnings in those terms: before you refer to opium as *kuro*, think about whether you want to affect the role of an insider to the world of drug-dealing.

Japanese Street Slang is a delightful book in which to browse—each example could be a line in the middle of a very entertaining movie, and one can hardly help imagining those nonexistent movies as one reads. It provides enough amusement to be an excellent Christmas present for one's friends (though probably not for one's parents). But it is also so phenomenally rich a source of information about the Japanese language that is otherwise inaccessible to *gaijin* (the most common Japanese term for occidentals—I like to translate it as "long-nosed, round-eyed, hairy barbarian") that it should be on the bookshelves of any serious translator of modern Japanese fiction and of any library that has even a small collection of books on the Japanese language.

Much of both the value and the fun of *Japanese Street Slang* comes from Constantine's extremely apt English translations, which reproduce with remarkable accuracy not only the content of each Japanese example but the connotations of nonchalance, flippancy, annoyance, anger, or disgust that are apparent in it. It is a shame that earlier dictionaries did not have on their staffs a writer/translator with Constantine's formidable skill at conveying the "register" of a translated example; perhaps then the 1927 edition of *Kenkyusha's Japanese-English Dictionary* would have translated *Kuso demo kue* (literally, "Eat shit") not as "A fig for you" but as the far more accurate "Go fuck yourself." Among the beneficiaries who will especially profit from *Japanese Street Slang* are the writers of subtitles for Japanese films, who will find in Constantine's translations ideal models for many of the lines in gangster movies and low-life comedies that they might otherwise have been hard put to translate.

Constantine informs me that the examples that he presents in *Japanese Street Slang* correspond to only a small part of the copious information that he has gathered about how the members of subcultures at and beyond the fringes of polite Japanese society speak, and how the members of polite society speak when they aren't being so polite. I hope that the growing circle of Japanophile readers will demand that Constantine continue enlightening and entertaining them by sharing more of the contents of his filing cabinet with them in sequels to *Japanese Street Slang,* and by replenishing his filing cabinet through more of the highly productive linguistic field research that made it possible for him to write *Japanese Street Slang.*

> James D. McCawley
> Professor of Linguistics and of
> East Asian Languages and Civilizations
> University of Chicago

INTRODUCTION

Japanese Street Slang sets out to accomplish two basic tasks: first, to paint for the first time a detailed and uncensored panorama of the rich body of forbidden Japanese—the kind of language that no dictionary would dare print; and second, to attempt, by analyzing the more private, jealously guarded secrets of modern Japanese speech, to present more realistic portraits of men and women from different walks of contemporary Japanese life.

When I began writing this book many of my Japanese friends and several scholars expressed horror at what one summed up as "washing our dirty clothes in public." The general consensus was that "foreigners should not learn bad language," often followed by: "and anyway, we don't have any bad language!" The lexicographer and linguist in me rebelled against this unscientific stance. It was proving to be a major hurdle in my initial research. Wherever I turned I encountered friendly Japanese faces gently declaring: "We do not say such things in Japanese." It was this denial that drove me to hunt through the seediest Japanese establishments, tape recorder in hand, ready to catch bad words. I was not prepared for what I found.

The biggest obstacle was the sense of privacy that seems to be instinctive in all Japanese. Is it a mechanism used to shield foreigners from contact with *warui kotoba*, "bad words"? This little stratagem has duped many a Japanologist into believing that the Japanese language is deficient when it comes to powerful and provocative slang. My initial expectations were summed up by a line in Jack Seward's *Japanese in Action:* "The Japanese lag behind us Westerners in the sheer beauty, sustained invention, and gasp-producing force of our native insults."

English slang still seemed to me the richest body of strong and direct language capable of a straightforward frankness unmatched elsewhere.

Wrong!

Once I began digging, Japanese street language started pouring in. My Japanese friends introduced me to their friends, who in turn introduced me to *their* friends. These people came from all walks of life: high school and university students; show business people of every shape, size, and description; gamblers and criminal elements—all contributed their shockingly vital and expressive language. My original intention had been merely to investigate swear words, but I was overwhelmed by the richness of Japanese street language.

My research leveled any remaining preconceptions. Time after time, the Japanese language came up with terms that were precise and unambiguous, razor-sharp in their specificity, words that could encompass a whole English phrase, sentence, or even paragraph. For example, English, along with its neighboring Western languages, boasts of thousands of risqué anatomical terms of a sexually explicit nature, but for the most part these are synonyms that, when it comes to actually describing these organs, turn on their puritanical heel and run.

Not so with Japanese. While formal Japanese is formidable at euphemism and understatement, Japanese street lingo is just as formidable in its frankness, abruptness, and uncanny punctilio.

To present the clearest picture of the capacity and scope of Japanese slang in the nineties, I decided not to limit myself to everyday slang and colloquialisms used and understood by the general population, but also to pry open the closed doors of Japanese subcultures to expose the jealously guarded private languages they use. When one considers the special properties of Japanese slang, an important national characteristic comes strongly to the fore. While in the West we like to think of ourselves as individualists, cultivating—to use a Japanese neologism—*mii-izumu*, "me-ism," the Japanese prefer to identify themselves with *uii-izumu*, or "we-ism." As Edwin O. Reischauer says in *The Japanese*: "The Japanese are much more likely than Westerners to operate in groups, or at least to see themselves as operating that way. Where Westerners may at least put on a show of independence and individuality, most Japanese will be quite content to conform in dress, conduct, style of life, and even thought to the norms of their group."

Belonging to a group or subculture in Japan means more than dressing alike, thinking alike, and acting alike as a manifestation of psychological commingling. In Japanese street culture, identifying with a group by way of language plays a more important role than it does in subcultures in the West. Students, Tokyo yuppies, juvenile delinquents, the police, the Yakuza Mafia, different criminal elements, groups involved in eccentric sexual behavior, all have their individual lingoes that border on jargon.

These varieties of slang serve to strengthen the "we-ism" bond of a group, to reinforce solidarity, and to exclude non-members, but they also play another important role: they provide the various street elements with specific terminology that standard language lacks. Words like these, which play such an important role in the complete picture of modern Japanese street slang, are known as *ingo*, or "hidden language." Like a real language, *ingo* is made up of many different dialects—in this case, lingoes—nurtured by the different street societies: pickpockets, thieves of every persuasion, and the sex business (which has its own specific subjargons, such as those used in Soapland massage parlors, strip and cabaret enterprises, prostitution rings, and the like). The *ingo* segment of street slang in Japan, unlike teen slang and *torendii* (trendy) speech, does not look West for linguistic inspiration. While the fashionable club set and the Tokyo crowd and young urban professionals all over Japan saturate their speech with American, American-inspired, or hybrid Anglo-Japanese expressions, the rougher street elements shun foreign-word imports and absorb the time-honored vocabulary of the crowd they identify with, often using words that sometimes reach back to street speech of the Edo period (1600–1867). Having gathered this hitherto uncollected body of Japanese, ranging from hidden and taboo language to the trendiest new expressions on the 1990 and 1991 scene, I set about my final task as detective-lexicographer, which was to shadow these words that are shunned and denied by standard speech and to pinpoint their etymological origin.

The Ins and Outs of Japanese Slang

Foreign words The most prominent general characteristic of modern Japanese slang is its reliance on Western languages, notably English, for inspiration and new words. These terms are known as *gairaigo*, "words from outside," and range from expressions like *haiteku*, (high tech) to *sūpā eirian*—"super alien," a teenage-slang expression used to comment on the ugliness of a girl (inspired by the extreme unsightliness of the extraterrestrials portrayed in films like *E.T.* and *Alien*).

The first foreign words to hit Japan were Chinese expressions which arrived with the first written characters brought by migrant scholars in the fifth century A.D. These characters and the words associated with them were for centuries revered as official and scholarly (much like the higher falutin' words of Latin origin in English).

In the meantime, the first Western influences were making themselves felt. In the 1540s the Portuguese arrived in Kyushu in Southern Japan, followed soon after by the Spanish. By the seventeenth century a Portuguese-Japanese pidgin seasoned with Spanish words had evolved in the port towns serving the booming trade (which, by the way, specialized in rifles). To this day Japanese has preserved words of Portuguese origin like *tempura* (from *tempero*, "flavoring"), *tabako*, "cigarettes" (from *tabaco*), *karuta*, "card games" (from *carta*, "card"). Spanish words still encountered colloquially today are words like the favorite sponge cake of Japan, *kasutera* (from *pan de Castilla*, "Castilian bread"), and *pan*, "bread," from the Spanish word *pan*.

The next torrent of foreign words to be absorbed by Japanese slang came from Dutch. In 1636 the military government of Japan, the Tokugawa shogunate, had forbidden all contact with the West, plunging Japan into a virtual isolation that was to last until the Meiji reform of 1868. Throughout these two centuries only the Dutch managed to keep a trading post open, in Nagasaki. The Nagasaki dialect readily absorbed many Dutch expressions from the colorful Netherlandic-Japanese pidgin that evolved in the port, and these then found their way into standard speech. Many Dutch words have survived to this day, like the slangy *otemba*, "romp" or "tomboy" (from *ontembaar*, "untamable"), or the now standard words *biiru*, "beer" (from *bier*), and *garasu*, "glass" (from *glas*).

The big boom came with the Meiji Restoration in 1868, when after two centuries Japan's doors were flung open to the West. This brought a flash flood of Western words and ideas. Some fanatics were so enthusiastic for all things foreign that there was even a serious movement to abolish the Japanese language altogether. Fascination for the Roman alphabet and its possibilities started the trend in Japanese slang, popular to this day, of using letters as substitutes for words. Some early examples are *U* for *ūman*, a Japanese pronunciation of "woman"; *B.A.*, pronounced *bi-ei*, for *baba*, "old woman"; and *S*, pronounced *esu*, standing in for "singer," meaning in this case "geisha."

The establishment of a strong Japanese navy before the turn of the century brought in another influx of foreign words, especially into the red-light districts of the major Japanese ports. Some of the more granular imports from American and British ports were *go taimu* (go time), the duration of a sexual encounter; *nambā* (number), to experience more than one climax (and by extension its verb form *nambaru*, to have more than one orgasm); *shōto* (short), a quick sexual experience, as opposed to an all-nighter; *sukuriin* (screen), for the hymen; and *sutan* (stand), for erection.

While red-light-district slang was receiving its first major injection of foreign words, the Meiji "in crowd" developed its own slang, notoriously fortified with newly acquired English terms. Expressions like *ōrai*, as in "all right," spread like wildfire, even attaching themselves to Japanese words, resulting in expressions like *ōrai geisha*, "all-right geisha"—a geisha whom we'd describe today as "an easy lay." Some of the terms adopted by Japanese from Western languages were exotic even to a Western ear (as is still sometimes the case). One notorious example is the word *kame*, referring to the European lap dog that became the rage in Japan during the Meiji period. (In popular novels of the time, every fashionable heroine had a charming little *kame* or two). This modish Meiji word is said to have originated when a Japanese overheard a foreigner say "Come here!" to his European doggie.

Dialects

Over the centuries slang fashions have migrated through different dialects. When, for instance, Kyoto was the capital (until 1600), the Kansai dialect was dominant and was imitated throughout the nation. The current Japanese idiom began to take shape during the early seventeenth century, when the Government was moved to Edo, today's Tokyo. By the end of the eighteenth century the Tokyo dialect had usurped the Kyoto dialect.

Today's regional dialects, often mutually unintelligible and bristling with uniquely local terminology, offer an important source of inspiration for Japanese slang. The modern Osaka and Kyoto dialects have provided mainstream slang with many trendy expressions, like *Aa shindo!*—"Man, I'm beat!," or *Mō akimahen!*—"I've had enough!" This new trend among younger speakers has been popularized by the mass media, especially comedians from the Osaka area, and has been baptized by Japanese linguists *shin hōgen*, or "new dialect," of which there are many examples in the text.

A particularly prominent one is the particle *jan*. *Jan* is a contraction of *ja nai*, which is itself a contraction of *de wa nai*, an informal form of *de wa arimasen*. All of these mean "it is not" or, depending on intonation, the tag "Isn't it?" or "Right?" The slangy *jan* most frequently acts as an emphatic affirmation, as in: *ii jan!* (Awesome!), *Torendii jan!* (Cool, dude!), and *Kimi no kuruma jan?* (It's your car, right?).

Jan originated in Nagoya and spread into the neighboring dialects of Shizuoka, Yamanashi, and Nagano, until it reached Yokohama, where it became a mega-hit in downtown Yokohama slang—so much so, that in the following years it became identified nationwide as Yokohamian. *Jan*'s final ascent to national stardom started in the late seventies and early eighties, when Tokyoites and other trend-conscious speakers started using *jan* as a send-up of Yokohama speech. By the late eighties and early nineties, *jan* was here to stay.

The other prominent dialect feature that will be encountered throughout the book is the transformation of the diphthongs *ai, oi,* and *ae,* in rough speech to the drawn-out vowel sound *ē.*

> *Shitai* (wanting to do) → *shitē*
> *Sugoi* (super) → *sugē*
> *Omae* (you, or yo!) → *omē*

Another phenomenon that has started recently in Tokyo is the shortening of words (inspired by neighboring dialects such as Fukushima and Yamagata):

> *Wakaranai!* (I don't understand!) → *Wakannai!*
> *Tsumaranai!* (Boring!) → *Tsumannai!*
> *Shinjirarenai!* (I don't believe it!) → *Shinjinnai!*

The Grammar of Rudeness

Japanese is a language with many levels of diction. For our purposes, we can say that it uses two scales for measuring relations between speakers. The first runs from extreme politeness to extreme rudeness; the second from extreme formality to extreme intimacy. Consider some of the ways of saying "(someone) is doing (something)," using the verbs *suru*, "to do," and *iru*, which forms the gerund.

Shite irasshaimasu (honorific)
Shite imasu (neutral, polite)
Shite iru (informal; used among friends, often in the contracted form *shite'ru*)
Shite agaru (offensive, pronounced *shiteyagaru* or *shiyagaru*)

Suru itself has two additional levels, *nasaru*, which is an honorific form of *suru*, and *yaru*, which is its rude or extremely intimate form.

Finally, an extremely polite form exists in which the honorific *o* is attached to the verb stem, which is followed by *ni naru*.

Nouns as well as verb forms change in response to levels of politeness. The sentence "He/She is reading a book" can serve as an example of all these different levels.

Hon o oyomi ni natte irasshaimasu. (Extremely polite and formal)
Dokusho o nasatte irasshaimasu. (Very polite and formal)
Dokusho o shite irasshaimasu. (Polite and formal)
Dokusho o shite imasu. / Hon o yonde imasu. (Neutral and formal)
Dokusho o shite iru / Hon o yonde iru. (Neutral and informal)
Hon o yondeagaru. (Rude)

Japanese slang usually opts for the ruder and rougher levels of speech.

Pronouns

In talking to others the choice of pronoun is also important; in fact, the very *use* of a pronoun is a choice in level of politeness, since pronouns are avoided in polite speech whenever possible. To use one at all is to shift your speech toward the informal and intimate.

A special feature of saying "I," "you," "he," "she," or "it" in Japanese is that some pronouns are used exclusively by men (or *very* tough women), and some by women (or men wishing to sound feminine).

I, me

Watakushi. Formal, polite, respectful. Used by both sexes.

Watashi. Usually feminine.

Atashi. The popular, casual, feminine form in everyday speech.

Atai. Very casual and feminine, used primarily in rough, slangy speech. Its Tokyo dialect variation *atē* has an even rougher edge to it.

Boku. The masculine equivalent of *atashi*, used in casual conversation by boys and younger men.

Ore. The rougher, tougher, masculine "I" especially favored in slang.

Washi. Preferred by older men, it is thought by many to be somewhat unsophisticated and provincial.

You

The Japanese pronouns for "you" are often considered too direct and are thus avoided in polite situations. Another option is to use the person's name.

Anata. Formal and, depending upon the context, somewhat feminine. When used by a woman to a man it can even be translated as "darling," though it is also used between middle-aged men in formal business speech or discourse. The contracted form *anta* is rude and masculine, though tough women use it too.

Kimi. Masculine, casual, and familiar in tone when used among men, and with a rough edge when used by men to women. (And a *very* rough edge when used by women to anyone except children.)

Omae. Masculine and familiar to the point of roughness. Pronouncing it *omē* makes it even rougher.

Temae. Often pronounced *temē*, is rough and too aggressive to use in most situations. *Temē* is especially violent when used to call somebody. It is analogous to the American expression "Yo!" or even "Yo! Asshole!"

He, She

The most respectful reference to a third party in Japanese is *kata* (person) prefaced by *kono* (this), *sono* (that), or *ano* (that, farther away). In everyday conversation, *hito* is substituted for *kata*. These polite and socially safe forms do not appear in the text of this book, as they are rarely used in street slang.

The other two standard words for "he" and "she" are *kare* and *kanojo* (like the English "he" and "she," they can seem rude if used in the presence of the person one is discussing). The Japanese versions of "he" or "she" that one is most likely to meet on the streets of Japan are the abrupt *koitsu, soitsu,* and *aitsu* (stronger than the English "this guy," "that guy," and "that guy there"). They are used only in the most casual circumstances.

It

Even "it" can be expressed more and less politely. A "thing" is a *mono* in polite, neutral speech, but it becomes a *yatsu* in rougher talk and street slang.

Particles

Standard particles such as *wa, ga,* and *o,* and the question particle *ka* are often left out in slangy speech (as you will notice in the example sentences throughout the text). Other particles, however, play a very important role in masculine and feminine speech, especially in slang.

Feminine particles

No at the end of a sentence in casual speech is generally considered feminine, but nowadays is becoming more unisex:

> *Iku no?*
> You're going?
> *Itsu suru no?*
> When are you going to do it?

Ne and *nē* as interjections at the end of sentences convey the meaning "right?" or "isn't it?". They are generally considered feminine, but are often used by men.

Wa and the slightly more emphatic *wa yo*, when used as particles at the end of a sentence, are one of the most distinguishing features that mark casual feminine speech.

> *Ii wa.*
> Okay.
> *Jōdan ja nai wa yo!*
> It's not funny!

Masculine particles

Na and *nā* are generally a rough and masculine sounding version of *ne* and *nē* .

Ze and *zo* are final particles used in rough, masculine, slangy speech. (*Very* few women use them.)

> *Ii zo.*
> Okay then.
> *Ore no da ze!*
> This is mine!

In slangy, informal speech men frequently end their sentences with the copula *da* plus an emphatic *ze, zo*, or the less strong *yo*. Women rarely use *da* in this way unless they are deliberately adopting male speech or are elderly and very provincial.

A Note on Romanization

In this book, a modified version of the Hepburn system has been used. *N* becomes *m* before *b*, *p*, and *m*. All long vowels, regardless of their Japanese orthography, are indicated by macrons. An exception is the long *i*, transcribed *ii*.

There is no consensus on the rules for dividing or joining Japanese words. For the purposes of this book, Japanese words resembling prefixes and suffixes, which modify the root term, have been hyphenated to make it easier for the reader to recognize the term being discussed. Prefixes such as *do-*, *kuso-*, and *chō-* and suffixes such as *-ppoi*, *-teki*, *-mitai*, *-kusai*, *-chikku*, and *-me* are all examples of these linguistic elements.

Apostrophes play two roles: they indicate contractions, such as *shite'ru* (for *shite iru*) or *itte'n* (for *itte irun*); they also mark the semantic and pronunciation distinction between a final *n* and an initial *n* plus vowel, as in *shinin*, "dead person," and *shin'in*, "true cause."

ACKNOWLEDGMENTS

All the examples in this book are actual contemporary Japanese slang as it is spoken in different sections of modern Japanese street society. I overheard some of these examples myself in the past year in Japanese bars and clubs, but most of them came from my many Japanese friends and acquaintances. I am extremely grateful for the invaluable linguistic and cultural information that they provided on the specific elements of Japanese society (criminals, the red-light district, pornography, and drugs) that they are conversant with. Due to the sensitive nature of their work, many of these individuals wish to remain anonymous.

I would like to express appreciation to Terumi Y. for the endless hours of help and guidance that she offered me in this project. Her long experience in the Tokyo red-light district, and the hours she spent sifting through contemporary Japanese pornography of every kind and description did much to illuminate opaque practices in contemporary Japanese society.

I am especially grateful to Wakako I. for checking the Japanese examples and for providing the voluminous information on school and university slang. Her deep interest in Japanese inspired me to probe more deeply into the etymology of these slangy and controversial expressions.

I would also like to thank Ryota I. for his help and information in shaping this book. I am especially indebted to him for his frank, open-minded discussions of terms and their usage, and for his help in analyzing modern expressions of dialect origin; Yoko K. for the information on the language used by today's motorcycle gangs and more mature street criminals; Kazu and Taka for their information on the Japanese drug trade and its language; Naoko for her invaluable help in identifying words of Osaka, Kyoto, and Nagasaki extraction, and for her help with teenage slang; Yukio, who, thanks to his extensive involvement in the Tokyo and Osaka red-light districts, was able to supply me with many intriguing anecdotes and expressions; and Christine H., a Westerner who was born, raised, and educated in Japan in a Japanese family—the only truly bicultural person I have ever met—for her many interesting and objective observations on all things Japanese.

I would especially like to thank Professor James D. McCawley for his invaluable help and advice. I would also like to express my thanks to Raphael Pallais for his enthusiastic support and to Mark Peterson for his help with American slang. I am also very grateful to the staff of the Oriental Division of the New York Public Library for their friendly scholarly assistance.

Finally, I'd like to thank all my friends at Meiji University who stalked the streets of Tokyo on the lookout for the most *torendii* street slang.

A Warning

Many of the Japanese expressions featured in this book are extremely potent.

Beware of using them inadvertently—mass panic might ensue.

JAPANESE STREET SLANG

A

AI. Love.

Ai is not a word to be taken lightly. It corresponds to the luminous Greek term agape—spiritual love as opposed to eros, or sexual love, which is *koi* in Japanese.

The word *ai* was imported from China by way of Korea during the Asuka period (538–710) by migrant Chinese and Koreans who brought with them the first written characters to Japan. (The same character is used in Chinese, pronounced *ai* in Mandarin, and in Korean, pronounced *ae*).

Ancient and distinguished as *ai* is, it turns up in all walks of Japanese life, especially in its verb form *ai suru*, "to love."

> *Ai shite'ru yo!*
> I love you!
> *Anta dareka ai shite'n no? Kao ni dete'ru yo!*
> You're in love with someone, right? It's written all over your face!

A cautious Japanese will try to avoid *ai* if possible, as the very force that renders it so compelling can backfire, making the speaker sound too pushy or too desperate. So, for safer casual chats about love, *suki*, "like," and *daisuki*, "really like," often prove to be more prudent choices.

> *Anta atashi no koto suki ja nain deshō! Tada atashi to netain deshō!*
> You don't love me! All you wanna do is sleep with me!
> *Daisuki da yo!*
> I love you!

3

The two standard Japanese words for lover are *aijin*, "love person," and *koibito*, "beloved person." Of these, *aijin* is the more potent expression, referring to the person that a married man or woman is having an illicit affair with. *Koibito*, on the other hand, is used as casually as "boyfriend" or "girlfriend" in English.

> *Aitsu no nyōbo Yokohama ni aijin ga iru rashii ze.*
> It seems his wife's got a lover in Yokohama.
> *Anata no koibito dare?*
> Who's your boyfriend?

In everyday Japanese slang one specifies boyfriends and girlfriends by turning the personal pronouns *kare*, "he," and *kanojo*, "she," into nouns: *watashi no kare*, "my boyfriend" (literally, "my he"), and *boku no kanojo*, "my girlfriend" (literally, "my she").

> *Nē! Anta ima no kare to kekkon suru no?*
> So, are you gonna get married with the guy you have now?
> *Ore no kanojo 'tte beddo de sugēn da ze! Omē ni misete yaritē yo na!*
> Man, my girlfriend's ace in bed! You should see her!

Another slang term favored in casual conversation is *kore*, "this," an expression invariably accompanied by a hand movement designating the sex of the lover in question. A fist with a raised thumb (the nail facing away from the speaker) indicates a male lover, while a fist with a raised little finger (the nail facing the speaker) indicates a female lover.

> *Atashi kanojo no kore kinō michatta.*
> I saw her boyfriend yesterday.
> *Omē kon'ya omē no kore to dekake'n no ka?*
> You going out with your girl tonight?

One of the in words for lover with the fashionable city crowd is the English "lover," which the Japanese pronounce *rabā.* In Japanese, the word is used exclusively for male lovers.*

> *Nē! Ano ko ga anta no rabā da nante iwanai de yo! Kawaii jan! Yaru jan!*
> Don't tell me he's your lover! Ooh! He's cute! Good for you!
> *Atashi ima rabā inai kedō, ima boshūchū na no!*
> I don't have a lover right now, but I'm on the lookout!

Two hot foreign imports that have become as common with younger speakers as *kare* and *kanojo* are the English *bōifurendo,* "boyfriend," and *gārufurendo,* "girlfriend."

> *Eee!? Anta no bōifurendo nijūgo! Chotto toshi ja nai?*
> Your boyfriend's twenty-five? That's a bit old!
> *Ore no gārufurendo tsumannē! Okimari no sekkusu shika dekinē!*
> My girlfriend's so boring! All she's into is regular sex!

The newest and zaniest Japanese synonyms for lover come from the high-school crowd, where a whole arsenal of code letters has been invented to facilitate covert risqué conversation and to specify the exact nature of the "lover" in question. For example, *eru,* for *L,* stands for lover; *esu efu,* or *S.F.,* is short for the more venturesome "sex friend"; and on top of the pile, the infamous *efu emu,* or *F.M.,* is short for "fuck mate," or in plain English, "piece of ass."

> *Nē? Ken ga Suzuko no eru da 'tte shitte'ta?*
> Tell me! Did you know Ken was Suzuko's lover?
> *Ima made nannin esu efu ita?*
> How many guys have you done till now?
> *Soko ni iru onna mita ka? Aitsu ga ore no atarashii efu emu da ze!*
> Did you see that woman there? She's my new piece of ass!

---

*To be used with circumspection, as *rabā,* "rubber," is gaining widespread acceptance as an up-and-coming term for condom.

ASOKO.   The sexual organs.

Asoko, "over there," is Japan's number one expression, used by old and young, to refer to male or female private parts. *Kanojo no asoko*, "her over there," can mean "her vagina," "her clitoris," or the whole sexual organ, while *kare no asoko*, "his over there," might refer to "penis," "testicles," or both.

> *Nureta asoko.*
> A wet pussy.
> *Aitsu no asoko ga chiisai/ōkii.*
> His thing's small/large.
> *Aitsu no bikini wa pichipichi dakara, asoko ga mieru.*
> Her bikini's so small you can see her thing.
> *Boku no asoko ga gingin tatchatta.*
> My thing got rock hard.

Another important word to know is *mono*, "thing." While *asoko*, "over there," is used for all sexual organs, *mono* is limited to the male genitalia because it carries the connotation of a tangible, solid object.

> *Oi! Ore Ken no mono shawā de michimatta yo! Kyōdai!*
> Man! I saw Ken's thing in the shower! It was humongous!
> *Atashi ima made kare no mono mita koto nakatta yo.*
> I still haven't seen his thing.

Another roundabout reference to the male sexual organ is *are*, "that." (People shy away from using *are* to refer to the female organ because it is also a very popular synonym for a woman's period.)

> *Kanojo ga iru dake de, ore no are kataku narun da yo na.*
> When she's in the room my thing gets hard.
> *Anta no are iren'no? Tetsudatte ageru wa.*
> Can't you get your dick in? I'll help you.

B

BAKA. Idiot.

This is the most popular Japanese swear word. Everyone and everything can look, sound, or be *baka*. In Tokyo it has lost much of its original potency, as "damn" or "shit" have in America. Outside Tokyo, however, it often still carries its pristine meaning, so be careful, especially in Osaka, where it really means "imbecile" or "mentally deficient."

> *Baka jan!*
> What an idiot!
> *Baka yarō!*
> Stupid idiot!
> *Baka mitai!*
> That's stupid!

Over the centuries, *baka* has been written with many different characters. One of the more entertaining compounds uses the two characters *ba*, "horse," and *ka*, "deer," legend having it a foolish king of the ancient Chinese Qin dynasty, upon seeing a deer, fatuously said *ba* instead of *ka*, and thus was the first to have earned himself the nickname *baka*. Its first appearance in writing was during the fourteenth century in the tales of the *Taiheiki*, but some scholars have traced it back to Heian-period (794–1185) words like *waka*, and *wakawakashii* (pronounced today *bakabakashii*, "idiotic"), both meaning "infantile," or "simple-minded."*

---

* The actual etymology of this word is highly disputed by Japanologists. The most widely held view is that it was imported centuries ago through Chinese from the Sanskrit word *moha*. Another

Baka yamerō yo!
Don't be such an idiot!
Baka yatte'n ja nē yo!
Cut the crap!
Baka itte'n na yo!
Don't talk shit!

Other derivatives of *baka* are *baka-chin* and *baka-mono*, both meaning "stupid guy."

Nan da ano baka-chin no chūsha no shikata!! Doko de menkyo hirotte kitan da?
Look how this moron parked his car!! Where did he buy his driver's license?
Omē tada no baka-mono da! Damare!
You're such an idiot! Just shut up!

Some of the favorite terms for "idiot" in Japanese slang today started off as provincial expressions originally introduced into mainstream speech as vigorous new insults. The favorite among these is *aho*, which originated in Osaka, but now ranks among the leading playful imputations of idiocy that Japanese can boast of. *Aho*, analogous to the American "stupid klutz!" or "moron!," is often used in Tokyo slang in Osaka syntax:

Omae aho ya de!
Man, you're a moron!
Sekkusu no tochū de onara o suru nante, omae aho da na!
You mean you farted while you were having sex! Man, you're a real moron!

---

school of thought links *baka* to the Ainu work for idiot, *paka*, while more eccentric authorities believe it to be of Indian extraction, related to the Hindi insult *bakwa*, the Bengali *boka*, or even the Malay *bakok*. The most creative group of all staunchly believes the term *baka* to be consanguineous with Bacchus, the god of wine, who, they claim, after a cup or two too many, was prone to *baka* behaviour. (See Yamanaka Jōta, *Kokugo Gogen Jiten*.)

Omē mata kuruma no kagi nakushita 'tte! Kono aho!!
You idiot!! You lost your car keys again!

When trendy Tokyo high schoolers wish to discuss idiots in private, they often employ cryptic codewords that serve to pixillate prying ears. One of these terms on the current scene is the simple *ei eichi ō*, from *A.H.O.* (which on closer scrutiny turns out to be our Osaka word *aho*).

Omē honto ni ei eichi ō da na! Atchi ike yo!
What a ying yang! Just get away from me!
Atarashiku kurasu ni haitte kita futari no otoko honto ni ei eichiō!
The two new guys in our class are such idiots!

Another Osaka term for idiocy popular throughout Japan is the melodious *ahondara*, a combination of *aho*, "idiot," and *dara*, a stronger form of *tara*, an emphatic Kansai-dialect suffix. The *ahondara* is a slow-witted, dull imbecile.

Ahondara ya de!
What an idiot!
Mō atashi ame no naka sanjikan matte'ta no yo! Kono ahondara!
You idiot! I waited for you three hours in the rain!

Another popular insult on the streets is the notorious *tawake*, originally imported from the Nagoya dialect. It was created from the verb *tawakeru*, "romping around." In Nagoyan it was used of brash and brazen individuals. Its modern meaning has expanded to include idiots of all degrees, shapes, and sizes.

Kono kurasu tawake bakkari da! Saitei da yo!
This class is fulla boneheads! It's disgusting!
Atashi Ken nanka suteta yo! Anna baka na tawake nan da mon!
I dumped Ken! He's such a stupid idiot!

The other favorite provincial insult on the street is *nōtarin*, made up of *nō*, "brain," and *tarinai*, "lacking." It had featured

9

in many regional dialects—Ashikaga, Tochigi, Oyama, and Kanuma—before it went on to nationwide stardom.

> *Ano nōtarin dete itte kurenai ka na! Atashi tsukarete'n no yo ne!*
> I wish that airhead would leave! I'm tired!
> *Uchi no otōto honto ni nōtarin da yo! Nanimo wakatte 'nai!*
> My brother's such an airhead! He's totally spaced out!

Another older popular insult targeting weak brains is *usunoro*, a term that originated at the beginning of the Taisho period (1912–26) and is a conflation of the words *usui*, "weak," and *noroi*, "slow."

> *Ano usunoro mata chikoku! Michi machigaettan da 'tte yo!*
> That lamebrain was late again! Can you believe he got lost?
> *Aitsu ga mata shiken ni ochita 'tte atarimae da yo! Usunoro dakara!*
> I'm not surprised he failed his exams again! He's such a lamebrain!

Another out-of-town hit now unfortunately past its prime but still often heard in hard-core street circles is *otankonasu*, which first appeared in the Utsunomiya, Ashikaga, Sanno, and Tochigi dialects.

> *Ore anna Shibuya kara kita yō na otankonasu-me to shōbai nanka shinē ze!*
> I don't want any dealings with that jerk from Shibuya!
> *Ore sonna kingaku de sono otankonasu shinyō shinē ze! Senshū no ikken oboete'ru darō ga!*
> I wouldn't trust that jerk with that kinda money! Remember what happened last week!

Another interesting term favored in hardened street circles is *ampontan*. It came to the big city from the Tochigi dialect, but speculation has it that it actually originated from the Chinese medicine *han gon tan*, also known as *ahotan*, "idiot medicine," a purported cure for depression and mental illness.

> *Ie no kagi o nakusu nan 'tte, omae wa honto ni ampontan da!*
> You're a real idiot, losing your housekeys like that!
> *Kono ampontan ga saifu o nakushita no wa sandome da zo!*
> This yo-yo has lost his wallet three times already!

Two of the less suave expressions popular today on the Japanese street are *shiri-nuke* and the somewhat stronger *ketsu-nuke*, both meaning "ass-less." Both were imported from the Ōtowara and the Utsunomiya dialects.

> *Dete ike! Kono shiri-nuke-me!*
> Get outa here! You fuckin' jerk!
> *Pāti ni ita ano onna dare? Nanka ketsu-nuke jan!*
> Who was that woman at the party? What a total jerk!

BŌSŌZOKU. Motorcycle gang.

The Chinese characters *bō sō* mean reckless driving, and *zoku* means tribe or gang, describing the bands of carousing juvenile delinquents that are a common phenomenon in Japanese cities. In the 1980s, Tokyo's National Police Science Research Institute estimated that over 42,500 youths were delinquentizing in over seven hundred gangs nationwide—most of them drop-outs from the regimented and highly competitive Japanese schools. What gives the *bōsōzoku* its specific character is the mode of transportation. At the bottom is the *zoku*, the poor-boy street gang, which has no transportation and does its harassing on foot. In the middle is the motorcycle gang, which is the most common. On top we find something uniquely Japanese: the rich bad boys with their car gangs. They paint their vehicles in aggressive colors, often attaching metal teeth, fists, and claws to the hoods. They race about the neighborhoods, brandishing streaming banners and flags out the windows, more bark than bite.

> *Zoku ni hairu.*
> To join a gang.
> *Kono bōsōzoku wa Heruzu Enjeruzu mitai.*
> This bike gang looks like the Hell's Angels.

What distinguishes these gangs from their counterparts in the West is their rigidly organized structure. They charge membership fees, chant slogans and gang anthems, and proudly wear badges and uniforms. Rigid behavior codes are enforced. Paradoxically, in attempting to escape from the straitjacket of Japanese schooling, these 42,500 youngsters submit to the absolute regimen imposed by the gangs.

The leader of the *bōsōzoku* is the *atama*, "head," or the *banchō*, literally "top number," while the second in command is the *sabu*, as in "sub-leader."

> *Yabē! Atama kuru zō!*
> Watch it! The leader's coming!
> *Atarashii banchō dare?*
> Who's the new head?
> *Sabu no baiku te o tsuketara, korosareru zo!*
> If you touch Number Two's bike, he'll kill you!

The regular gang members are the *ningen*, "humans," the *shatei*, "brothers," or the *heitai*, "soldiers":

> *Omē! Ima nannin ningen irun dai?*
> Hey, how many are in your pack now?
> *Ore-tachi Saitama no shatei to ima igamiatte'run da yo!*
> We've been clashing with the Saitama punks!
> *Bōsōzoku no heitai kuru zo! Zurakare!*
> The guys from the motorbike gang are coming! Let's split!

BŪBŪ. Fart.

This expression conveys rumbling gastric sounds, and the onomatopoeic *būbū iu* means to complain. The equally onomatopoeic *būbū suru*, however, means to fart, so be very careful. A slight grammatical error on your part could induce a red-faced silence or raucous laughter.

> *Onara būbū suru.*
> To fart sonorously.
> *Onara būbū shinaide yo! Kusē kara na!*
> Man! Don't fart, it stinks!

Another crass but cheerful word for farting is *būsuka*.

> *Omae beddo no naka de būsuka suruna yo! Kusakute tamannē yo!*
> Don't fart in the bed! God, it stinks!
> *Ojii-chan'ttara!! Onegai dakara! Okyaku-san no iru toki būsuka shinaide chōdai!*
> Grandpa!! Please! I wish you wouldn't fart when we have guests!

You can repeat *būsuka* twice in order to give a break-wind description the extra edge.

> *Onara o būsuka būsuka shita.*
> He let one rip.
> *Atashi oto ga denai yō ni shita tsumori datta no ni, sugoi būsuka būsuka dechatta yo!*
> I thought it was gonna be a discreet little fart, but I really let one rip!

To bring home the full effect of a drawn-out fart, use *būsuka* four times in quick succession.

> *Onara o būsuka būsuka būsuka būsuka shita!*
> He farted loud and long!
> *Ore imo kutta kara to omoun dakedo, hitobanjū būsuka būsuka būsuka būsuka demakuri nan da yo!*
> It's those potatoes I ate! All night I've been farting away like crazy!

BUSU. Ugly.

This is the worst insult that can be hurled at a Japanese girl. It covers American expressions like "dog-face" and is at its most potent when hissed viciously as a drawn-out, sibilant *MM–busss!!*

The etymology of this very popular word is a controversial and much-debated mystery among Japanese scholars. Kittredge Cherry, in *Womansword*, suggests that *busu* was a poison derived from aconite root. A person ingesting the poison would die with a face grotesquely contorted in agony; hence the association. I hold to the view that *busu* is a direct borrowing from the indigenous Ainu language of northern Japan, from *pushu*, meaning ugly.

> *Nan da kono busu!*
> What a dog!
> *Busu dakedo, ii hito dakara.*
> She might look like shit, but she's a good person.

Hakike ga suru hodo, or *ōē suru hodo*—"enough to make you vomit"—can be used to add spice to *busu*.

> *Suzuko wa ano doressu de hakike ga suru hodo busu datta!*
> Suzuko looked so bad in that dress that I almost barfed!
> *Nani sono kamigata! Ōē suru hodo busu da yo!*
> What's with that hairstyle? You look like shit!

Teenagers recently invented the secret code *H.B.*, pronounced *eichi bii*, for *Honto ni Busu* (really ugly).

> *Ano eichi bii mita ka yo? Ōē⁻!*
> Did you see how incredibly ugly she was? Puke!
> *Ore no imōto sugē kompurekkusu motte'run da yo! Nanise eichi bii dakara!*
> My sister's got a complex 'cause she's ugly!

Tii-Bii-Esu, for T.B.S., is also popular in schools for singling out ugly classmates and is more flexible in meaning in that it can be used for boys as well as girls. It stands for either *Totemo*

Busaiku na Shōjo—a totally unpleasant girl—or *Totemo Busaiku na Shōnen*—a totally unpleasant boy.

> *Ano tii bii esu, jibun no koto nan da to omotte'n darō?*
> Who does that ugly troll think she is?
> *Aitsu chotto tii bii esu da kedō, demo are, ne, totemo jōzu na no yo!*
> He might not be much to look at, but elsewhere he's pretty good, if you get what I mean!

When the film *Alien* hit the Japanese cinemas in 1980, the extreme ugliness of the extraterrestrial being inspired the term *eirian* as a cutting remark about a girl's looks.

> *Aitsu no kanojo eirian!*
> His girlfriend is an ugly dog!
> *Eirian mitai na kao shiyagatte, mukō e ike!*
> Fuck off, you freak!*

The English prefix "super" (pronounced *sūpā* in Japanese) gives the appellation *eirian* that extra forcefulness, as does *do-*, a popular slang prefix of Osaka provenance (from the Tokai dialect) that intensifies words it precedes.

> *Omae no suke sūpā eirian da zo!*
> Man, your girlfriend's a total dog face!
> *Mattaku, ano do-eirian dō yatte anna ii otoko te ni ireta no ka nē?*
> How the hell does a total freak like her get her hands on such cute guys?

BŪ!

This is a feisty new form of negation inspired by the loud buzz signal used in popular Japanese T.V. game shows when the poor contestant chooses the wrong answer.

---

* Literally: "You have a face like an Alien! Get away!"

Anta nampa shita? Bū!
Did you get lucky?
(Thumbs down)

Kanojo beddo de yokatta?
Bū!
She good in bed?
(Thumbs down)

Its opposite is *pinpon* (usually pronounced playfully and chirpily as *pin-pōōn*). This comes from the merry cornucopian gong that heralds victory in the game-show world.

Kinō onna to dekita?
Pinpōōn!
Did you get laid yesterday?
(Thumbs up)

Are ga anta no kuruma ja nai?
Pinpōōn!
Isn't that your car?
(Thumbs up)

Another new "yes" in the Tokyo club scene is the super-cute *yāpi!*, which should be sung out about an octave higher than one's usual speech pitch. Originally thought of as being too feminine for male usage, it is increasingly becoming a unisex expression.

Atarashii dorama o mita?
Did you see the new soap?
Yāpi!
Yessiree!
Ne, kondo no kare 'tte sugoku kawaii jan!
Yāpi!
Your new boyfriend's real cute!
He sure is!

C

CHAMPON. Mixing different types of alcoholic drinks.

In Japan drinking with one's colleagues often becomes a social obligation. As round after round is amicably imbibed, *champon*, the mixing of different types of alcohol, is likely to happen. The inspiration for this expression came from the noodle dish Nagasaki *champon*, which is made up of different types of meats and vegetables. The source of this word is the mixture of sound that the traditional Japanese percussion instruments *kane* (bell) and *tsuzumi* (drum) make when played together. The *kane* is responsible for the tinny sound *chan* and the *tsuzumi* for the sonorous *pon*, creating the rhythmic compound *champon-cham-pon*.

> *Champon suru.*
> To mix drinks.
> *Uisukii to biiru o champon shitara, sonna ni waruku nai to omou.*
> I don't think that mixing whiskey and beer is all that bad.

CHARAMPORAN. Irresponsible, flaky.

"The sense of responsibility weighs heavily on the Japanese of all classes. Hence the desire to evade as much of it as possible." (Daniel Crump Buchanan, *Japanese Proverbs and Sayings*)

Of the main expressions for irresponsibility, *musekinin* (irresponsible), *sekininkan no nai* (without a sense of responsibility), and *ate ni naranai* (unreliable), the slangiest is *charamporan*, which has only recently graduated to dictionary status.

The source of this word is the expression *chara*, meaning "to lie." In the 1920s the expression *chara hora* (literally, "to lie a lie") became fashionable. Over the years its meaning shifted. To brighten the phrase, *h* became the more pleasing *p*, emphatic *n-ms* were attached at the end of each unit, and *charamporan* was born.

> *Charamporan na yatsu.*
> An irresponsible dude.
> *Charamporan na koto suruna!*
> Don't do such a flaky thing!

CHICHI. Breasts.

The Chinese character for *chichi* carries the connotation of suckling or breast feeding, an idea which passed down into modern colloquial speech to become the most popular Japanese word for what in America are called "tits" or "boobs." Breast fixation, especially partiality to larger breasts, is a recent phenomenon in Japan. Only two generations ago no eyelashes were batted when farm girls of all sizes and dimensions worked topless in the fields; the massive postwar Westernization brought an end to that.

> *Ōkii/chiisai chichi.*
> Big/small tits.
> *Kanojo wa buraja o tsukenai kara, chichi ga yure ni yureru.*
> Her tits bounce around 'cause she's not wearing a bra.

A new high-school slang word for girls with small breasts is *non-chichi*, a variation of which is *no-chichi*.

> *Kawaii kedo, non-chichi!*
> She's cute . . . but no tits!

Aitsu nani-sama da to omotte'n da yo? No-chichi no kuse ni!
Who the hell does she think she is? She doesn't even have
any tits!

Zō chichi, or elephant boobs, is usually used nastily by
teenagers in reference to obese girls, but can also be used in
admiring appreciation of a girl's uncommonly large breasts.

Kanojo zō chichi no kuse ni yoku anna bikini kireru yo na!
How can a fat cow like that wear such a bikini?
Nanda ano zō chichi! Sugē kyōdai!
Look at those tits! Humongous!

Chichi kurushii (short for *chichi aikurushii*, literally "pretty
boobs") is a denomination of male esteem and appreciation for
a woman's physical attractions, much as "nice piece of ass" is
in American English.

Oi! Miro yo ano onna! Chichi kurushii ze!
Hey! Look at that babe! Her tits are killers!

CHIKAN.   Pervert, molester.

In crowded places such as Tokyo busses and subways during
the rush hour there often lurks a *chikan*, a molester who will
stealthily approach an unsuspecting victim. This encounter is
called *chikan ni au*— "encountering a molester."

The word is made up of *chi*—the Chinese character for
madness or derangement—and *kan*—suggesting a large,
strong man. A typical verbal reaction to being molested is
"Kya! Chikan! Tasukete!" (Yuck! Pervert! Help!), or simply
"Chikan!"

Ano hito chikan mitai.
That guy looks like a pervo.
Atchi ikanai hō ga ii yo! Chikan darake da yo!
I wouldn't go there! It's teeming with perverts!

The female counterpart of the *chikan* is the *onna no chikan* or the *chijo*. She is the woman who touches or rubs against men in crowded areas. *Chi*, as in *chikan*, means insane or crazed; *jo* means woman.

> *Mata ano chijo ore no asoko sawatte kita yo!*
> That nympho touched my thing again!
> *Mata asa ano chijo ni atchatta yo!*
> That nympho approached me again this morning!

A wide miscellany of eccentric sexual behavior can be rendered by adding the suffix -*ma*, (evil spirit, devil, or demon) to words that run the gamut from enema to razor blade.

The *ashiname-ma*, "foot-lick demon," is a foot fetishist who enjoys licking feet during, or as a substitute for, sex. The equivalent term in American fetishist circles is "toe-licker" or "foot-licker."

The *chikuri-ma*, "pinch devil," approaches his victims (usually female) and squeezes or pinches their bottoms, legs, arms, or breasts.

The *gōkan-ma*, "rape-devil," is the rapist, and thus the most dangerous individual suffixed with a *"ma."*

The *kamisori-ma*, "razor devil," enjoys making incisions in women's clothing, usually in the cramped quarters of the rush-hour subway.

The *kanchō-ma*, "enema demon," is an individual who likes receiving and in some cases giving what in Japanese fetish circles is called an *ero kanchō*, an "erotic enema."

The *kutsuname-ma*, "shoe-lick devil," is the shoe fetishist, who enjoys licking a partner's shoe, usually in a grovelling, submissive stance.

The *nozoki-ma*, "peeping demon" is a voyeur who uses binoculars (often under the guise of being a nature enthusiast) to observe people doing things like dressing, bathing, or engaging in sexual intercourse.

The *sawari-ma*, "touch devil," will usually slip his hand "inadvertently" up skirts in crowded areas for a quick fondle.

CHIKUSHŌ! Beast!

In a situation where your average American would say "darn!," "damn!," "shit!," or "fuck!," your average Japanese would say *chikushō*! (beast), *baka*! (fool), or *kuso*! (shit). If a Japanese is asked offhand "What is the worst Japanese word you can think of?" more likely than not *chikushō* will come up.

Crass though it might be, *chikusho* and related expletives can sometimes be used in polite surroundings—as long as they are muttered to oneself.

> *Chikushō! Saifu o wasurechatta!*
> Damn! I forgot my wallet!
> *Chikushō! Shippai shichatta!*
> Shit! I made a mistake!

Other inelegant expletives to be expressed sotto voce are:

> *Nan da kor'ya! What (the fuck)'s this!*
> *Nan da koitsu?* What's with him/her?
> *Nani yo?* What the hell?
> *Nan da yo?* What the hell?

Safer expletives to keep in mind are:

> *Mattaku!* Well I never! Really! (literally, "altogether, entirely")
> *Masaka!* No! Impossible! It can't be!
> *Oya, maa!* Dear me! Oh my!
> *Komatta na!* Oh darn! (lit. "This worries me!")
> *Ar'ya!* I never!

CHIMPIRA. Punk.

The *chimpira* is the aggressive young delinquent found in high school yards, motorcycle gangs, or at the bottom of the Yakuza (Japanese Mafia) hierarchy.

21

The origin of the word *chimpira* is in dispute. Generally it is believed to have developed from *chimpo*, penis, but Taka Hōryū in his work *Kotoba no Yūrai* suggests that *chin* (m) comes from *kin*, meaning gold, and *pira* comes from *hira hira*, meaning "flimsy." The idea is that punks might look slick and glittery on the surface, but take away the clothes and the attitude and you are left with nothing.

> *Nande aitsu no musuko wa chimpira ni narisagacchimattan darō na? Bon bon na no ni nā!*
> I wonder why his son ended up as a punk? Rich kid, too!
> *Zurakare! Ano chimpira-tachi naifu motte'ru ze!*
> Let's split! These punks have knives!

Another common term for juvenile delinquent is *machi no shirami*, "town louse," or gaining now in popularity, *shirami*, "louse," for short.

> *Atashi yoru ni dearuku no kowakute, machi no shirami darake nan da mon!*
> I'm afraid of walking out at night! This area's fulla hoods!
> *Kono hen ni hataraite'ru onna wa minna ano shirami-tachi o kowagatte'ru.*
> All the girls working in this neighborhood are terrified of those hoodlums.

Two other current slang words, *marubo* and *marubi*, refer to an extremely rough and dangerous punk. *Maru* suggests the idea of "label" or "stamp," while *bo* or *bi* (in this case the initial "B") stands for *bōryoku*, violence. These punks have what we might call "violent with a capital *V*" stamped on them.

> *Ore no itte'ru gakkō marubo darake de, sugē abunē!*
> My school's just teaming with punks! It's fuckin' dangerous!
> *Kono marubi renchū keimusho ni hairu beki da ze! Abunakute shōganē!*
> These hooligans should be stuck in jail! They're dangerous!

CHINCHIN. Penis.

This expression has a playful, childlike quality to it, which makes it useful in colloquial speech as one of the few direct references to the male sexual organ that is too cute to be crass. *Chinko, chimpo, chimpoko,* or its inverted form, *pokochin,* are other conveniently euphemistic terms that may be used judiciously in mixed society, if circumstances call for a direct but playful reference to the penis.

> *Chiisai/ōkii chinchin.*
> A small/large pecker.
> *Aitsu wa chinko o shiko shiko suru.*
> He's playing with his pecker.
> *Tatta chimpo.*
> A hard dick.
> *Chimpoko no atama.*
> A dick head.
> *Pokochin marudashi de uro uro!*
> He's wandering around with his dick hanging out!

Recently, much to everybody's surprise, *chinchin* broke out of its masculine semantic confines when the Saitama Board of Education decreed it to be the only acceptable term for vagina in elementary school sex-education classes. For years *ochinchin* (literally, honorable pecker) has been the official elementary-school word for penis. Unfairly enough, the Japanese language has no term of an equivalently euphemistic caliber for vagina. Perplexed teachers were resorting to terms like *opampom,* or dubious words fashionable in the red-light district like *wareme-chan* (literally, Miss Crack). The burning debate at school-board meetings focused on establishing an agreeable word for vagina, a word that would not offend the delicate sensibility of a preteen girl (boys are excluded from official sexual enlightenment until much later). When the *ochinchin* edict was passed, many teachers were too relieved to lodge official complaints about the oddity of this solution, although some individuals voiced concern as to whether young ladies in the year 2000 would know an *ochinchin* from an *ochinchin*.

Back in down-to-earth circles you might hear *dekachin* in reference to a large, well-proportioned sexual organ. *Deka* (from *dekai*) means huge and is a popular word that was adopted from the Osaka dialect.

> *Aitsu no asoko wa dekachin da na!*
> His thing's like a ramrod!
> *Kare no dekachin dakara, hairu to saikō yo!*
> He's hung like a bull! He drives me crazy when he puts it in!

Furuchin, "wagging penis," and *yokochin moreru*, from *yoko kara chimpo ga moreru*, "the penis escapes from the side," are two terms used for inadvertant penile exposure.

> *Sonna furuchin no mama de arukimawaranaide yo!*
> Don't walk around with your dick hanging out like that!
> *Hayaku mite! Aitsu yokochin morete'ru!*
> Quick, look! His dick's hanging out!

CHIRŌ. Coitus "un"-interruptus.

A man who after an unnaturally long sex session is still going strong with no climax in sight is labeled in Japanese as a *chirō*—a "slow leak" (the character *chi* means slow and *rō* means to leak).

> *Kare chirō dakara, owatta ato sugoi tsukaren no yo ne.*
> My boyfriend takes such a long time to come that I'm always wasted afterwards.
> *Kare 'tte honto ni chirō de komatchau! Iku no ni nijikan mo kakarun da mon!*
> He's *so* slow in bed! Sometimes it takes him two hours to come!

A neologism on the Tokyo high-school scene is *yojigen no shōnen*—the fourth-dimension boy. This synonym for *chirō* pictures the man afflicted with the tendency to coitus "un"-interruptus as caught up, or suspended in, a "fourth dimension."

> *Atashi kinō hitobanjū yojigen no shōnen to yatta! Mada asoko ga itakute, itakute!*
> Yesterday I was doing it all night with this long-haul-ball guy! My thing's still hurting!
> *Kare 'tte honto ni yojigen no shōnen da wa! Hitobanjū yatte'ta no!*
> He takes so long to come! We were doing it all night!

CHITSU. Vagina.

This is a term for vagina that ranks with *joseiki* (female sexual organ) in formality. It is favored in anatomical textbooks and medical circles, but is considered by many to be too punctilious for everyday conversation.

However, in Japanese, technical terms like *chitsu, sōnyū* (insertion), or *anaru sekkusu* (anal sex) can prove enticing, especially in the red-light district. The technical term often offers the most direct and thus the crudest way of calling a spade a spade—giving a speaker the opportunity for a witty touch of erudition among all the obscenities being uttered.

> *Chotto kyō chitsu ga itai no yo ne! Yarisugi kashira?*
> My vagina kinda hurts today! Maybe I got too much action!

Less technical terms from the raunchiest sectors of the red-light district show an inspired creativity: *Moya moya no seki,* "the hairy barrier"; *kemanjū,* "hairy bean jam bun," similar to the American expression "hair pie" or "fur pie"; *nikumanjū ,* "meat bun"; or *kuma no kawa,* "bear's fur"—used for especially hairy women.

Even if you are visiting the most profane Tokyo sex club, be extremely careful not to slip and inadvertently use one of the above expressions. And if you hear them, duck and run—you are in dangerous company!

> *Ore ga ima hoshii no wa kemanjū da.*
> What I need now is some snatch.
> *Chotto matte'te! Ima nikumanjū aratte kuru kara sa!*
> Wait for me here! I'm just going to wash my twat!
> *Kono nozokibeya wa moya moya no seki miru made ikura haraun darō?*
> How much do we have to pay at this peepshow before we get to see some snatch?

CHONGA. Bachelor.

The expression *chonga* has had a long and colorful journey from Korea of the middle ages to modern Japan. The original word was *chon-gag*, a traditional knotted hairstyle worn by Korean boys and unmarried men. As tradition gave way to Western influence, young Koreans cut their hair American style, and the word *chon-gag* became the accepted Korean term for bachelor. On the eve of World War II the Japanese government mobilized an estimated six million Koreans under the national service draft ordinance. Many of the Koreans brought to Japan as forced laborers or military draftees stayed after the war to become the largest ethnic minority in Japan. These people brought with them a plethora of Korean words that found their way into colloquial Japanese. Korean influence on street slang grew stronger in the Japanese underworld as powerful Yakuza-Mafia gangs (like the Toseikai, or "Voice-of-the-East Gang") of ethnic Koreans were established. Ethnic Koreans mixed words of Korean origin into their speech, creating jargon impenetrable to outsiders. Some examples:

Banchoppari. Mixed-blood Korean-Japanese.
Enyon. Derogatory word for a Japanese woman.
Gejashiku! Asshole!
Haraboji. Old man.
Kyonchari. Policeman.
Sannomu. Idiot.
Somunomu. Idiot (literally, islander)
Uenomu. Derogatory word for a Japanese man

Chonga is one of the Korean words that broke the linguistic and social barriers that kept these words underground. It became one of the most popular slangy words in Japan for the unmarried man.

Chonga dakara sa!
Well, he's a bach!
Chonga seikatsu 'tte, nanka ii yo na!
Bachelor life is great!

A recent linguistic trend allows for pinning down an out-of-town *chonga* in a snappily humorous way by adding the first syllable or two of his hometown to *chon*:

Fukuchon. A bachelor from Fukuoka.
Narichon. A bachelor from Narita.
Sachon. A bachelor from Sapporo.
Sakachon. A bachelor from Osaka.

D

DANI. Good for nothin'.

The word *dani*, or "tick" (the bug), is the downtown Tokyo equivalent for the American loafer or good-for-nothing. A *dani* has no steady job, gambles, and might do a bit of pimping on the side. Like a tick, he lives off others.

> *Aitsu hakkiri 'tte dani mitai na yatsu!*
> That guy looks like a total good-for-nothing!

Danidachi, "tick's friend," is the word for blackmailer or leech.

> *Ore wa omē ni yaru kane nanka ichi mon mo nē! Kono da-nidachi!*
> You're not getting a dime from me, you dirty leech!

Another term for "no-good dude" is *himo*, literally "string." Similar to *dani*, it is used for someone who is a gambler, a loafer, and an idler, but its main connotation in Tokyo slang is "pimp."

> *Aitsu wa sannin no onna no himo nan da 'tte sa.*
> That pimp's got like three women working for him.
> *Nanka, himo mitai na yatsu dakara, hataraku koto wa shinai!*
> Man, this dude's like a pimp, he never works!

In the same class we find the *aburauri*, "oil seller." The inspiration for this word came from *abura o uru*—"selling oil," a long-standing idiom for wasting time—as the oil seller in olden times used to stroll leisurely from house to house chatting, flirting, and gossiping.

Doko de abura utte kita no, konna osoku made?
Where were you loafing about so late?
Aitsu wa oya no kane bakkari tsukau, aburauri da!
This guy lives off his father's money, what a loafer!

DANKON. Penis.

This word literally means "male root." It is a Sino-Japanese loan word that is not much used in colloquial speech, but has become a favored expression in contemporary pornography. In the sixties it gate-crashed the world of literature when the controversial poet Shiraishi Kazuko published a poem titled *Dankon*. A sample: *"Dankon wa hibi ni gun gun sodachi"* (The man root grows larger day by day).

Outside modern poetry, the current usage of *dankon* conforms to the established contemporary pornographic format:

Aitsu no gin gin tatta dankon.
His hard, throbbing man root.

And to very casual red-light district conversation:

Atashi dankon wa shaburanai!
I don't suck dick!

The characters *dan*, "male," and *kon*, "root," are the Chinese reading (*on yomi*) and can also be pronounced in their native Japanese (*kun yomi*) rendition, creating another uncouth word for penis: *otokone*.

Anta no kare no otokone don'gurai dekai no?
So, how big is your guy's dork?
Atashi kagiana kara kare ga otokone ijitte'ru no michatta!
When I looked through the keyhole I saw him playing with his cock!

Other plant motifs in Japanese words for penis are *rakon*, "bare root," meaning "cut" or "circumcised" penis; *yōkei*,

30

"male stem"; and *hine daikon*, "shriveled radish," used to describe small wrinkled penises.

> *Ara! Ima made yatta kimpatsu no otoko minna rakon datta yo!*
> You know, all the foreigners I've done till now had cut dicks!
> *Ano onna ni totte, ichiban miryoku-teki na tokoro ga yōkei yo!*
> All this woman is interested in is dick!
> *Bikkuri shichatta! Ano ō-otoko konna ni chitchai hine daikon motte'n da mon!*
> I was so surprised! Such a humongous guy with such a shriveled little dick!

DARASHINAI ONNA. Loose woman.

A contraction of *darashi no nai*, the dictionary definition of this expression is "slovenly, untidy, slack, or loose." For a woman to be labeled *darashinai* implies that she has wandered from an accepted mode of ladylike comportment. It might be an accusation of slouching, dragging her feet, or even drooling, but more often than not it is an indirect accusation of loose morals.

> *Kaminoke o chan to tokashinasai! Darashinai onna ni miemasu yo!*
> Comb your hair properly! You look like some tramp!
> *Atashi nande aitsu ga darashinai onna bakkari tsurete'ru no ka wakannai.*
> I don't get why he always hangs out with such cheap girls.

A direct accusation, tantamount to calling someone a "slut," is *megumi no ko*, "girl of happiness."

> *Ano megumi no ko wa pappa sannin mo irun desu 'tte!*
> I hear that tramp has like three sugar daddies!

There are coarser expressions that become very specific in a physical way. A woman who has many sexual partners is referred to as *hirogeru onna*, "(thigh-)spreading woman," or *sugu hirogeru onna*, "immediately (thigh-)spreading woman."

> *Maiban chigau otoko to nete, hirogeru onna no suru koto!*
> You're acting like some kinda nympho, sleeping with different guys every night like that!
> *Aitsu sugu hirogeru onna dakara, ippatsu yatte miro yo!*
> She's such an easy lay! Go for it!

In the same class we find *mae o kasu*, "lending out the front," and *shirigaru*, "light-assed."

> *Ano ko wa mukashi kara zutto mae o kasu onna nan da yo.*
> She's always been a tramp.
> *Sonna ni mijikai sukāto o haite aruku to, shirigaru onna ni miraremasu yo.*
> Everyone is gonna think you're some tart if you walk around in a such a short skirt.

DASU. To ejaculate.

The verbs *dasu*, "to send" or "to throw out," *deru*, "to come out," and *iku*, "to go," are the three most common expressions for ejaculation, parallel to "coming" in America.

To announce an orgasm one can either use the verb in its short dictionary form or add the suffix *sō* (literally, "it seems like" or "I'm about to"):

> *Iku . . . iku!*
> I'm coming . . . I'm coming!
> *Ikisō da!*
> Wow, I'm about to come!
> *Itta?*
> You came?
> *Desō!*
> I'm coming!
> *Chikushō! Desō! Desō!*
> Oh shit! I'm coming! I'm coming!

Mō dashita? Saitei!!
Oh shit! You already came?
Anta naka de dasanaide yo!
Don't come inside me, O.K.?

A risqué synonym for the above verbs is *buppanasu*, "to totally let go," which is equivalent to "shooting one's wad" or "getting one's rocks off."

Ore kinō buppanashita toki, mō owari ka to omotta!
When I shot my wad yesterday I thought I was gonna die!
Aniki ga buppanashita toki, monosugē oto ga shita kara minna ni kikoechimatta!
My brother was making so much noise when he got his rocks off that we all heard him!

DEBU. Fat, fatso.

This is a nasty taunt similar to American expressions like "tub of lard" or "fat-ass."

Nan da kono debu!
Get a load of fatso!
Sonna ni taberun ja nai yo! Debu ni natchau!
Don't eat so much! You'll turn into a pig!

The verb form is *deburu*, to grow fat.

Aitsu honto ni debute'ru!
Man! He's really fat!
Dō shiyō? Mata debutchau!
What am I gonna do? I'll get fatter!

"To become fat" is expressed as *debutte kuru*.

Kenji, omae nanka honto ni debutte kita!
Shit, Kenji! You've really blown up!

Ano ko daietto shite'run ja nai no? Nande anna ni debutte kuru no?

Isn't she supposed to be on a diet! How come she's got even fatter?

The school of thought that subscribes to the "two tons are more fun" theory, and whose credo is "more bounce to the ounce and more cushion for the pushin'" is called in Japanese the *debusen zoku*, "fatso-partial gang," or *debusen* for short.

Ore wa debusen dakara ano zō chichi tamaranai!

I'm into lard, man! That ton of flesh there really turns me on!

Ore anna onna to dēto shinē yo! Ore no koto debusen da to omotten no ka?

I wouldn't go on a date with a woman like her! You think I'm into fat or something?

DEKA. Police.

Many of the informal references to the police force popular in Japan's streets today originated in the late-nineteenth century as Yakuza jargon. Words for police like *gacha, in'ya, ite, jinkoro, mappo, mambo, pēchan,* or *pēshan* started their careers as secret words in clandestine gangster talk, and have remained a part of the underworld lingo.

Ano gacha ore-tachi tsukamaeyō to shita kedo, umaku bakureta ze.

That badge tried to nail us, but we managed to get away.

Ki o tsuketa hō ga ii ze! In'ya nanka kagi tsukete'ru ze!

We'd better watch it, man! The boys in blue are onto us!

Kono hen no ite yarō, tondemonē kuso-domo da!

The fuckin' cops in this neighborhood are real assholes!

Shizuka ni shiro! Mambo ga iru!

Quiet! The law!

Konna ni pēshan uro uro shite'tara, ore biku biku shichimau yo!
I always get nervous when the fuzz are around!

"Mappo!" or *"Deka!"* as a warning once had the secretive quality that "Cops!" did when it was first used. The cover of some of these words was blown in Japan when gangster movies became the craze in the 1950s and 1960s. In America as in Japan, word formulas (like "spill the beans" or "hit man") that had been the exclusive property of hardened criminals were suddenly introduced into middle-class homes, cataclysmically expanding the average man's view of the world.

Deka ni kakawarun ja nē zo! Ki o tsukero!
Careful, man! Don't mess with the cops!
Ano mappo-me nani sama da to omotteyagarun da!
Who the fuck does that pig think he is!

DEKORU. To apply a thick layer of make-up.

By Western standards, Japanese women wear surprisingly heavy makeup. Nevertheless, the general consensus in Japan is that cosmetics should be subtly applied, enhancing the features without trying to significantly change them. New, extra-harsh Tokyo club-scene words like *dekoru* (from "decoration"), point the finger at transgressors.

Sonna ni deko deko dekotte mo, aitsu kimochi warui dake da yo!
She's slapping that makeup on by the pound, but she still looks like shit!
Ano kimpatsu no kyapi kyapi onna-domo iya ja nē ka? Anna ni dekotte yo!
Don't you just hate those foreign bimbos? The way they paint themselves!

On the high-school scene, sharp-tongued teenage girls are quick to lash out at any peer whose makeup is overly ornate with sarcastic expressions like *gokusaishiki*, "gorgeously colored."

> *Ano gokusaishiki no meiku shite'tara, otō-san ni korosarechau wa yo!*
> Your dad'll kill you if he sees you painted like that!
> *Suzuko baishunfu mitai! Anna gokusaishiki no kao shichatte sa!*
> Suzuko looks like a total whore with that makeup!

A recent arrival on the teenage-lingo scene is *faundēshon jiwa*, "foundation wrinkle," a taunt reserved for middle-aged ladies who over-indulge in makeup in the hope that it will rejuvenate their features, applying foundation so thick that there are cracks in it.

> *Nan da ano faundēshon jiwa, kyabasuke babā mitai da na!*
> Look at that makeup! She looks like an old slut!*
> *Kanojo anna ni faundēshon jiwa tsukurimakutte mo shōganai yo nē! Babā wa babā na no ni ne!*
> What's the point of all that paint? A hag is a hag!

---

* *Kayabasuke* is a popular nasty reference to red-light-district women. *Kyaba* is short for "cabaret" and *suke* is a derogatory *Yakuza* word for "woman."

E

ETCHI. H.

The initial *H*, pronounced *etchi*, is commonly used to judge something or someone as perverse. *KYA! Etchi!* (Oooh, gross!) is a characteristic reaction of horror when one is suddenly confronted with something sexually explicit. The *H* stands for the word *hentai* (abnormal, or pervert) or *hentaisei* (abnormal sex).

> *Etchi na koto suruna! Omae!*
> Yo! Don't be gross!

To add force to *etchi*, emphatic prefixes like the popular Osaka-dialect *do-* and the prefix *chō-* (super) can be used.

> *Ano kyabasuke do-etchi!*
> That bimbo's a total sleaze!
> *Ano eiga chō-etchi datta yo! Zembu marumie nan da ze!*
> That film was just *so* raunchy! You could see everything!

For a touch of wit, trendy speakers add American-derived intensifiers like *daburu*, "double," and *sūpā*, "super," to *etchi*, creating humorous and spicy international-sounding concoctions.

> *Hanashi kakenaide yo! Kono daburu etchi!*
> Don't talk to me, you total pervert!
> *Ano ko bājin no kuse ni sugē sūpā etchi nan dakara!*
> She's pretty kinky for a virgin!

Ekisutora etchi, as in "extra H," has developed into more of a compliment than an accusation:

Atashi no kare ekisutora etchi na no!
My boyfriend, he's *nasty!*
Kono doresu 'tte honto ni ekisutora etchi da yo ne! Sekkyoku-teki!
Ooh, that dress is nasty! Fierce!

Etchi suru, to do *H*, is a novel term for sexual intercourse, similar to slangy American terms like "doing the dirty deed," "getting down and dirty," or "doing the nasty."

Suzuko to etchi shita?
Did you lay Suzuko?
Etchi shiyō?
Shall we get down and dirty?

EMU. M.

The initial *M* can have various allusions in Japanese slang. *Emu*, for instance, can represent *musuko*, which means "son," and by extension is frequently used in street slang to refer to the penis.

Aitsu no emu chiisain da yo ne!
His dick's real small!

Emu is also used as an abbreviation for *masu*, which is itself an abbreviation of *masutabēshon*, "masturbation."

Emu shite'ru!
He's jerking off!
Hazukashikatta! Aitsu emu shite'ru toki ni, boku heya ni haitchatta kara!
Man, I was so embarrassed! He was beating his meat when I entered the room!

Emu-teki, "M-like," has two meanings. In the Japanese gay world it means "butch-looking" or "straight-acting," the *emu* representing the *M* of "masculine":

Atashi emu-teki na bōya hoshii no yo!
I want a butch boy!
Kare 'tte honto ni emu-teki na no! Atashi sore ga daisuki!
Ooh, he's *soo* butch! I love it!

In S&M circles, on the other hand, M means masochist.

Aitsu emu-teki na yatsu dakara.
He looks like he's a Mazo.
Bikkuri shichatta! Atashi ni muchi utte hoshii da nante, aitsu emu-teki datta no yo nē!
I was so surprised! He wanted me to whip him! He's a Mazo after all!

ERO. Porn.

Ero is short for *erochikku,* "erotic," and has been popular on the Japanese streets since the early Showa period, in the twenties.

As a Japanese prefix it has the same effect on nouns as the English "porn" or "sex."

Ero bide. Porn video.
Ero den. 900 number, or obscene phone call.
Ero fantajii. Sex fantasy.
Ero hon. Sex book.
Ero kanchō. Sex enema.
Ero kasetto. Sex tape.
Ero shashin. Porn photos.

The adjectival form of this prefix is *eroi,* meaning "obscene."

Omae eroi yatsu da zo!
You're so raunchy!
Eroi!
Gross!
Ano hon sugē eroi!
That book's really raunchy!

39

Another *ero* variation is *erochika*, a "totally cool" term from Japan's modern-day high-school scene for what American teens call a "pervo-geek" or a "sex-freak." The uninitiated bystander might be led to believe that "erotica" is being covertly discussed, but the etymology of this faddish neologism is the phrase *ero ni chikai*—"close to obscenity."

> *Anna erochika ni sawarasete tamaru ka! Jōdan ja nai!*
> I'd never let a sick dude like that touch me! No way!
> *Anta no otōto 'tte honto no erochika ni natchatta ne!*
> Your little brother's turned into a total sicko!

ESU. S.

The initial *S* has had a long and colorful history in Japanese slang. In the 1870s, when the opening of Japan instigated mass-hysteria for all things Western, the Roman alphabet began to be used as an exotic and secretive code. *Esu*, for example was to represent *shan* or *shen*, both Japanese pronunciations of the German word *schoen*, meaning beautiful. *Kanojo shen*, meaning "She is beautiful," was groovy and slangy at the time, and it soon metamorphosed into the more evasive *kanojo esu*. The next generation, in the first two decades of the twentieth century, created Anglo-German concoctions like *bakku-shen* (from back + *schoen*), originally meaning "nice ass" but later also "attractive from behind, but what a shock when you see her from the front."

Both these terms (which are still used by older slang speakers) were also rendered as the initials B.S., pronounced *bii esu*. In modern times this initial has been used expansively in all corners of Japanese slang to stand in for words like:

"Escape" (as in *S*-cape)

> *Ano gurūpu kara esu shiyō ze.*
> Let's split from that group.

Esu shinai to yabai ze!
Let's get the hell outa here!

"Smoking"

Koko esu eria?
Is this a smoking area?
Nē! Ima kara esu shinai?
You wanna have a smoke now?

"Secret"

Kono koto esu ni shit'oite yo.
Keep that a secret.
Kore zettai ni esu dakara ne!
This is a total secret, O.K.!

"Sex"

Kinō sando esu shita.
I had sex three times yesterday.
Esu wa dō?
How about a little fling?

"Sperm"

Esu no omorashi.
A blob of sperm.
'Yada omae! Esu no shimi tsukete! Kondo kara ki o tsukete yo!
Hey! You got a cum stain on this! Be more careful next time!

Sperm is also referred to in the contemporary high-school scene as *bitamin esu,* or "Vitamin S."

Kino no bitamin esu no aji wa yokatta yo.
I liked the taste of that cum yesterday.
Kare ga itta toki kare no bitamin esu sokorajū ni tobichitchatta no!
When he came, his juice spurted all over the place!

Esu, for "sister," refers to a very close friendship among young girls that might extend into the realm of lesbianism.

> *Ano ko-tachi itsumo beta beta shite'ru kara, kitto esu yo!*
> Those two girls are always all over each other. They must be lezzies!
> *Anta-tachi esu ja nai no?*
> You girls are gay, right?

The newest *S* arrival on the Tokyo scene is the *san esu zoku* (three *S* gang), referring to the group of clubby young socialites fitting the "three-S ideal" that elevates them to the realms of super chicness:

> The first *S:* *Sara sara no kami* (slick hairstyle).
> The second *S:* *Sube sube no hada* (super skin).
> The third *S:* *Sukkiri shita sutairu* (slim shape).

> *San esu zoku ja nai to ano kurabu ni hairenai yo.*
> If you're not one of the pretty people there's no way you'll get in that club.
> *Ken no pāti ni itara sokorajū san esu zoku darake de saikō datta yo!*
> Ken's party was super! The whole in-crowd was there!

F

FERA. Fellatio.

Japanese words for fellatio fit into two groups, foreign imports favored by the modern younger crowd and domestic words favored by maturer, or at least more conventional slang users.

Of the two groups, the foreign words (all of them now American or American-inspired) are gaining ground as, to Japanese ears, they have the triple advantage of being naughty, exotic, and ultra-fashionable.

Needless to say, fellatio stands at the top of the list of taboo subjects. If you look up fellatio in a very modern English-Japanese dictionary, *ferachio*, the Japanese transliteration of "fellatio," comes first as the only formal and popularly understood term. Then comes the obsolete and therefore inoffensive Japanese term *kyūkei*, which is made up of the characters for "suck" and "stem," followed by a punctilious explanation like *"Danseiki ni taisuru seppun,"* or "Kissing of the male sexual organ." In Japan today, the most widely understood word for fellatio is *fera*, a Japanese contraction of the English word. Often you will hear it in the form of *ofera*, the honorific *o* added as a coy form of linguistic shock-absorber.

> *Watashi ofera daisuki!*
> I love sucking dick!
> *Kono bā de hosutesu no fera no sābisu ari ka yo?*
> Do the girls at this bar offer fellatio service?

A popular word for fellatio that was recently invented in the Tokyo red-light district is *kyandē*, inspired by the English word "candy."

Suzuko no kyandē wa saikō!
Suzuko's blow jobs are the best!

Sakku nashi kyandē wa gomen yo!
No condom—no blow job!

Many of Japan's sex clubs, whose philosophy is to cater to the customer's every whim, have developed extraordinary fellatio techniques that appear on their "menus" under exotic American names. *Kokku sakkingu,* "cock sucking," *kokku-sakkingu purē,* "cock-sucking play," or *kokkusakkingu gēmu,* "cock-sucking game," for instance, imply a fellatio technique often performed with the hostess' mouth full of liqueur or sauces like ketchup. Other American-inspired expressions for fellatio like *ōraru sekkusu,* "oral sex," or *furūto,* "flute," are gaining popularity on the sex club scene.

Since AIDS claimed its first fourteen victims in Japan in 1985, the price of *nama* (raw, or in this case condomless service) has gone up, although to this day many Japanese still believe that AIDS only hits homosexuals and drug addicts. Either way, careful hostesses who use condoms on their customers have developed titillating techniques and acrobatics that come under the heading of *ofera kabuse,* "fellatio with cover." This includes slipping the condom on with their mouths so that it becomes a useful tool instead of a hindrance.

G

GEI. Gay.

This is a direct borrowing from the English "gay," meaning homosexual. It is a more recent arrival on the Japanese slang scene than the now well-established word *homo* which, by the way, has recently made it into the realm of dictionary respectability.

> *Aitsu gei?*
> He's gay?
> *Suimasen! Moyori no gei kurabu wa doko ni arimasu ka?*
> Excuse me! Where is the nearest gay club?

A *gei bōi*, however, is not a gay boy in the American sense of the word; a *gei bōi* or a *gei bōi-san*, "a Mr. Gay Boy," is a young man with effeminate airs who works in a gay club (more often than not in drag), serving and entertaining the customers regardless of his sexual preference.

> *Ken wa okama ja nai kedo, shigoto de gei bōi to shite hataraite'run da.*
> Ken's not really a faggot, he just works at a drag bar.
> *Chotto, ano gei bōi-san sannin yonde kurenai? Ato, shampen mo ne!*
> Get us those three "girls" there, will you? And champagne, please!

Clubs will have signs saying:

> *Gei bōi-san-tachi to enjoi shite kudasai.*
> Please enjoy yourself with the (Mr.) gay boys.

In recent student slang, *gei-chikku* helps point the finger at a man who is behaving a little more girlishly than custom sanctions. It is a saucy concoction inspired by the ending of the word *roman-chikku*, "romantic," and is at its most potent as an adjective.

> *Gei-chikku na yatsu.*
> A faggoty dude.
> *Gei-chikku na kaminoke.*
> A faggoty hairstyle.

In gay circles, boys who are definitely not gay are termed *nonke*, a contraction of *gei no kehai ga nai*, "no gay vibes."

> *Yappari nonke!*
> So he's straight after all!
> *Nande aitsu omae to netan darō? Aitsu nonke ja nakatta?*
> How come he slept with you? I thought he was straight?

A tough-looking homosexual and men who are into leather and bondage with other men are referred to in Japan as *hādo-gei*, "hard gay," or *hādo koa*, "hard core," which is short for *hādo koa gei*, "hard-core gay."

> *Ne, ne! Mite mite, onē-chan! Ano hādo gei wa oishisō ne!*
> Ooh! Girl! Take a look! That butch number's cute!
> *Ano futari no hādo koa, ittai dotchi ga dotchi de yarun darō?*
> Those two butch fags, I wonder who fucks who?

GENNAMA. Money.

When cash or money is discussed in Japanese everyday life, basic words like *okane*, "money," *genkin*, "ready money," or *kyasshu*, "cash," are used. On the streets, however, Yakuza jargon and slang favored by robbers, pickpockets, and other underworld cliques offer a colorful assortment of idioms inaccessible to the foreigner and even to the average Japanese.

Today the word *gennama* lies on the borderline of respectability, although until after World War II only the street crowd would have known or used it. Etymologically, it comes from *gen* (money), and *nama* (raw or fresh). It originated as an *ingo* (secret Yakuza slang) word during the Meiji Period (1868–1912) and led an underground existence until it entered popular usage through the cops-and-robbers films of the 1950s and 60s.

> *Gennama ima motte koi!*
> Hand over the cash now!

Many of the other words for money in use today on the streets and in the underworld originated in the Meiji or the Taisho period (1912–26). Words like *ura*, "back"; *tsura*, "face"; *higo*, "protection"; *riki*, "convenience"; and *watari*, "handing over," have remained street lingo used exclusively by thieves and pickpockets.

> *Ore no ura dakara!*
> That's my dough!
> *Tsura motte'ru?*
> Got any moola?
> *Omae no higo iranē zo!*
> I don't need your fuckin' cash!
> *Sono riki ore ni watasanē to, buchikorosu zo!*
> If you don't hand over the dinero I'll beat the shit outa you!
> *Shimpai suru na! Watari o tsukete kite yaru kara!*
> Don't worry! I'm gonna get the bread together!

Another word popular on the streets is the mysterious *ru*, as in:

> *Ru motte'ru?*
> You got the cash?
> *Ru chōdai!*
> Gimme the money!

Few users of this short, elusive word know its interesting background. The word that inspired *ru* was *nagare*, meaning flowing stream or current (the idea being that cash can flow like water). The ideogram for *nagare* has more than one pronunciation; *nagare* is the *kun yomi*, or native Japanese reading, while the *on yomi*, or Chinese reading gives us the obscure *ru*, a perfect candidate for a discreet code.

The exotic-sounding term *tsūpin* belongs to the same family of underground slang. It originated as a fusion of *tsūka*, "currency," and *pin*, "money."

> *Omae no tsūpin nante iranē!*
> I don't need your loot!
> *Tsūpin yokose yo! Soshitara ii butsu yaru ze!*
> You give us cash, we give you good stuff!
> *Ken ni tsūpin o yattara, sayōnara datta wa yo.*
> After I gave him my dough, Ken walked out on me.

Counterfeit money is known as *nisegane*, "fake money," or *nisesatsu*, "fake bill."

> *Ano baka yarō! Yaku to hikikae ni nisegane tsukamaseyagatte!*
> This fuckin' asshole gave us fake cash for the dope!
> *Shimpai suruna yo! Kono nisesatsu tsukaeru ze!*
> Don't worry! We can use these fake bills!

Bundles of fake notes (usually the top bill is real and the rest is plain paper) are known on the streets as *anko*, "bean jam," from the Japanese bean-jam buns that look like plain buns but have bean jam hidden inside.

> *Kore anko ja nai ka? Baka ni suru no mo ii kagen ni shiro!*
> Man! This is paper! Don't fuckin' fuck with me!
> *Hayaku koko zurakarō ze! Aitsu-ra ga anko ni ki ga tsuku mae ni na!*
> Let's get the fuck outa here before they catch on it's fake!

GOBŌ. Penis.

A *gobō* is a type of long, thin burdock root, light brown in color. In Japanese slang, words for roots and vegetables are often used to describe male genitalia. On the one hand, these words act as risqué euphemisms, while on the other they appeal by pinpointing with amazing accuracy the distinguishing features of a particular penis. These vegetables can distinguish subtle penile attributes and peculiarities such as size, texture, color, and length of foreskin with a specificity that the gruff resourcefulness of Anglo-Saxon slang can not even approach.

Another vegetable in this class is the *kyūri*, an indigenous Japanese cucumber, thin in shape and four to five inches long. This cucumber's width, length, and body is believed to reflect the proportions and the tactility of an average erect penis, and is therefore used in red light district circles to refer to a commonplace, run-of-the-mill penis.

The *imo*, "potato," can be used to refer to a shorter but fatter than average penis, while the *satsuma imo*, or "sweet potato," is larger but unshapely.

The Japanese *matsutake* mushroom is used for penises with slim long shafts and disproportionately large heads.

A small wrinkly penis can be referred to as a *hine daikon*, a dried radish.*

An uncircumcised penis with the head completely covered by the foreskin can be alluded to as a *rakkyō*, a pickled scallion.

GŌTŌ. Robber, burglary.

This is a vague but forceful word that the average Japanese and the media use to refer to either violent situations such as

---

* A village proverb often quoted by earthy grannies (usually followed by a loud cackle): *Monde ajidase hine daikon*—"You have to massage a shriveled radish well before it tastes of anything."

holdups, burglary, housebreaking, or plundering, or the actual gunman, burglar, housebreaker, or plunderer.

> *Gōtō ga haitte, heya o mechakucha ni shita!*
> A robber broke in and turned the whole apartment upside down!
> *Gōtō ga atashi-tachi no mono zembu totte itchatta no yo! Ze–embu yo!*
> This thief took everything we had! Ee–verything!

Ginkō gōtō (bank robber, or bank robbery), *kenjū gōtō* (a gunman, or a holdup), or *hōseki gōtō* (jewel thief) are some of the possible combinations in which you can find this term.

When criminals get together to talk shop, ordinary words like "thief" or "robber" prove to be too colorless and broad to be of any service. "What do you mean by 'thief'?," the confused specialist will ask "Are you referring to a push-up ghee, a lush roller, a second-story man, a spider, a chain man, or are we discussing a worm-walker?"

The Japanese criminal world is just as sensitive as its American counterpart when it comes to criminal job descriptions. Some of the types of thief and the cognomens that *ingo* (criminal language) initiates use to chat about each other are:

> *Agari*, "the ascender," is the individual who specializes in cat-burglary.

> *Aki*, "vacant," refers to the thief who will target a home only if its inhabitants are out.

> *Akinaishi*, "trade expert" is the master thief who has developed his art to a finely tuned perfection.

> *Akisu*, "snooper," is a term reserved for the stealthy, super-discreet purloiner.

> *Anatsutai*, "hole-enterer," can be either a general reference to thieves, or more specifically to one who specializes in breaking and entering traditional Japanese houses by making a hole in the outside wall.

Asarifumi, "hunt step," is the individual who specializes in thefts from unattended shopcounters.

Garasuhazushi, "the glass remover," specializes in the stealthy removal of glass in windows or doors as a mode of breaking and entering.

Genkanarashi, "the front-door smasher," is less subtle than "the glass remover." His or her specialty is to break down any doors that separate him or her from his or her objective.

Gui is a criminal argot word for accomplice, inspired by the word *tagui*, "of the same kind."

Ichimaimono, "one person," is the lone-ranger type of criminal who works alone, with no accomplices, no gang affiliations, and no reliance on connections.

Inaori, "the threatener," is usually used for a mugger.

Iri, "entering," is another *ingo* synonym for thief in general.

Itafumi, "floor step," is the thief who specializes in public-bath locker rooms, from which he will steal anything: soap, clothes, wallets, and jewelry. The root of this word, *ita*, "floor" or "floorboard," is used with various suffixes to create synonyms for locker-room thief such as *itabashiri*, "the floor runner" or *itanomikasegi*, "floorboard labor," sometimes pronounced *a la Osaka* as *itabakasegi*.

Kaikuri is a train thief whose method is to exchange bags that look alike.

Kajidoro, "fire thief," can be either an individual who sets fire to the place he intends to rob in order to profit from the commotion, or an individual who is quick to profit during disasters like fires, earthquakes, or typhoons.

Kanebako, "money box," is a train thief (*bako*, "box" is criminal argot for "train").

51

Kanekuchi, "money mouth," is a reference to the coin receptacle of a public telephone, and by extension an allusion to a small-time thief whose forte is ripping off phone booths.

Kanetataki, "money beater," is a mugger. The inspiration for this term came from the concept that this type of criminal will approach his victim in the street and threaten to "beat the money" out of him if he does not hand it over.

Kerikomi, "the kick enterer," is a synonym for burglar. If in English a burglar breaks and enters, the *kerikomi* specialist kicks and enters.

Kumo, "spider," is a cat burglar or, as American criminals would call him or her, "a spider."

Kyakushitsunerai, "guest-room aimer," is a thief who targets hotels, specializing in removing valuables from the rooms.

Nobi is another synonym for cat burglar, inspired by the verb *nobiru*, "to climb in."

Obu, "hot bath," is a public-bath or locker-room thief.

Ohayo, "good morning," is a train thief, who gets on the night train very early in the morning. During the customary refueling stop before its final destination, he or she ransacks the train and then hits the road.

Ohiki is the accomplice of a professional shoplifter whose function it is to create a diversion so that his partner will be free to work.

Okkake is a word for mugger that came originally from the Tochigi dialect. It was inspired by the verb *oikakeru*, "to follow."

Osae, "the restrainer," is the aggressive burglar who will stop at nothing to get at the goods.

Oshiiri, "pushing and entering," is another variation on the individual who breaks and enters.

Oshikomi, "pushing with force," is a synonym for the robber who pushes his or her way forcefully into a residence with the intention of plundering it.

Otenkinagashi, "the weather criminal," is the person who stands outside watching while his friends are inside looting.

Sewanuki is a word used for the thief who at night stalks the streets and bars looking for inebriated individuals to rob. This expression is made up of *sewa*, "to help," and *nuku*, "to pull out," since this thief holds out a "helping hand."

Shiro usagi, "the white rabbit," or just plain *usagi*, "rabbit," is an appellation reserved for the petty criminal. In olden days the "rabbit" thief would limit himself to stealing vegetables from the fields; today the expression has broadened to include all criminals who aim for minor-league targets.

Zumburi, "from top to bottom," is the locker-room thief who methodically cleans out locker rooms "from top to bottom."

GŪ! Good!

Every generation introduces its own favorite expressions for the word "good." What was "Groovy!" and "Neat!" a while ago in America became "Cool!" and "Way to go!" followed by "Organic!" "Orgasmic!" "Deadly!" "Stellar!" "Awesome!" and

"Totally awesome!" with a retro reinstitution in the 1990s of "Groovy!" and "Cool!"

In the same way, each new generation in Japan discards the previous generation's appreciative exclamations and institutes its own. Anyone in any way connected to Japan's in crowd of today avoids the following exclamations like the plague.

Ikasu! (to cause to go) is parallel to the "Swell!" or "Neat!" of three generations ago.

It was followed by *Kimatte'ru!*

Nau da! was the rage of the 70s. Its literal meaning was "It is now!"—*nau* taken directly from "now." This was followed soon after by *nauii*, an inspired transformation of "now" into an adjectival *"now-y,"* meaning "trendy," or "groovy."

The late 70s and early 80s saw *kakkoii!*, which hatched from the phrase *kakko no ii* (well-shaped, good-looking). It is still extensively used by no-longer-quite-so-trendy yuppies in their early thirties.

So what *is* awesome now in Tokyo? In the late 80s, *gū!* as in "good" became the total rage. It appeared in many different forms:

> *Sugē gū!* Totally awesome!
> *Mamosu gū!* "Mammoth good," popularized by the actress-singer Sakai Noriko.
> *Mechanko gū!* "Messed-up good!"
> *Mechakucha gū!* "Fucked-up good!"
> *Dan gū! Dan* is short for *danzen*, meaning "positively, absolutely."

Gū can also be used in its adjectival form *gū na*.

> *Gū na yatsu da!*
> He's a cool dude!
> *Gū na kuruma jan!*
> Awesome car!

The most recent arrival on the club scene is *Torendii!* or "trendy." Clothes, cars, friends, feelings, anything and everything "cool" can be labeled *torendii!*

Uaa! Aitsu torendii!
Wo! He's awesome!
Omae no kanojo sugē torendii!
Your girlfriend's really cool!
Kare no sutairu torendii!
That guy's smooth!

GUDŌ. The thief's tools.

Professional thieves are often master technicians who rely heavily on the finely tuned instruments they use for breaking and entering. If the American criminal's "black box" is filled with "coils," "can openers," "widgets," "jiggers," and the like, what will we find in the Japanese black box, you may ask. *Gudō* is the standard *ingo* (criminal slang) word for the burglar's trade tools, his "hardware," as we would say in the United States. It has the typical *ingo* characteristics of being a word inversion, in this case of the standard word *dōgu*, "tool." Some of the typical *gudō* on the streets of Japan are:

> *Ara*, meaning "knife," originated in the adjective *araarashii*, "rough." Its U.S. equivalents are "blade" and "chopper."
>
> *Ate*, "objective," is the name of the wrench or blade used for breaking in.
>
> *Emma* is a word for the pincers used for picking locks or other operations requiring delicacy. The word *emma* is of ancient Sanskrit origin (Yama). Emma is the King of Hell in Buddhist lore. The king's transmutation into a thief's pincers was prompted by Japanese mothers, who when a child is ill-behaved will all too often threaten that King Emma will come and do serious tooth-pulling.
>
> *Hajiki* is the favorite underworld term for "gun," stemming from the verb *hajiku*, "to flick" or "to flip."

Kanejū is the special fine wire used for prying doors open. The word evolved from the characters for *hari*, "needle," which is made up of two components. If you break the character apart, the left component is *kane* ("metal" or "money") and the right component is *jū* ("ten").

Kani, "crab," is the name of a small pair of scissors useful for snipping through bag straps or cutting into outside pockets to reach otherwise unapprochable valuables.

Oisore, "at a moment's notice," is a sharp little knife that can be put to use for all types of propitious thieving, not to mention its handiness as a weapon of defense in times of need.

Ōtomachiku, "automatic," is the automatic that some criminals keep on them just in case.

Pachinko is another popular thief-jargon word for "gun," inspired by *pachinko*, the Japanese pinball game in which the players have to hit the balls.

Saka is the knife of any shape or size that might be found in a Japanese thief's black box, suitable for anything from cutting and prying things open to self-defense. The word *saka* was inspired by Osaka, a city renowned by knife enthusiasts for its high-quality output.

Shippiki is a sharp precision tool convenient for picking locks.

Teikurō is another synonym for the gun that the prudent larcenist keeps in his box. It comes from a famous Kabuki play in which the hero Teikurō gets shot mistakenly.

Unagi, "eel," is a thin rope that comes in handy in a multitude of situations.

GYARU. Gal.

The 90's have given birth to new Japanese "gals" of the most astonishing variety. Tokyo's backstreets are suddenly bustling with new species of young women that have only recently been discovered and classified: "Cinderella flight" girls, "Daddy" girls, "Uncle" girls, "Bell trot" girls. When it comes to girls, you name it, modern Tokyo has it!

Ā-pā gyaru. The foolish girl. This girl is considered modern but foolish. Modern because she falls for every man who propositions her, and foolish because she is not clever enough to cultivate a steady relationship.

Bairin gyaru. The "biling"-girl. The "biling"-girl is a trendy girl in the international sense of the word. As the pun on bilingual suggests, she is not limited to one tongue. The "biling"-girl has traveled, possibly studied abroad, and can hold her own in any social setting. Only one *gyaru* can upstage her, the rare *torairin gyaru*, the "triling"-girl, who can chat in not two, but three tongues.

Goji made gyaru. The until-five girl. This girl is a new brand of office girl. She is not particularly interested in her job, and at the stroke of five—the end of the work day—drops everything and bolts from the office. Closely related is the *berusasa gyaru* (the bell trot girl), who, when the bell rings at the end of the working day, trots.

Oban gyaru. The auntie girl. This type of girl lags behind the times and can't face up to the fact that Japan is entering the twenty-first century. She shies away from all the modern airs that her sisters cultivate and seeks refuge in mannerisms more becoming to a middle-aged matron than someone fresh out of her teens.

Ofukuro gyaru. The mom girl. The mom girl is closely related to the auntie girl, the main difference being that mom girls are more assertive, and like to fix, organize, arrange, and mother everyone and everything in sight.

Ojin gyaru. The geezer girl. This girl is believed by many to be a dangerous new phenomenon. First, she is not girlish. On top of this, she hangs out in bars frequented by middle-aged men, cultivates gruff manly speech, smokes, holds her liquor well, and in general has what are regarded as mature, masculine interests in Japan—drinking, golf, and an aggressive interest in the opposite sex.

Oyaji gyaru. The dad girl. The dad girl, like the geezer girl, is also deficient in girlishness. She is assertive and brusque and makes a point of bullying her friends, be they boys or girls, as only a father could.

San nai gyaru. The triple-no girl. Many Japanese believe that this new feminine phenomenon is an indication of the decline and fall of modern society. The generation of the 80s believed that girls either married or, if worse came to worst, sacrificed themselves to their careers. The *san nai gyaru*, a phenomenon of the 90s, is different: She refuses to sacrifice herself to anything. She says no to work, no to marriage, and no to having children.

Shindarera furaito gyaru. The Cinderella flight girl. This girl is also brand new. She is a moneyed, professional girl who seeks adventure on weekends by going alone or with girlfriends on bargain package tours to misbehave in neighboring countries like Guam or Hong Kong.

For boys who will not be boys when they ought to be, *gyaru* can be used as a sobering slap on the wrist. The *gyaru bōi*, or "girl-boy," is a sensitive boy who has feminine mannerisms and girlish interests. *Gyaruo-kun* (Mr. Girl) is a spicy new term made up of *gyaru* (girl), *otoko* (man), and *kun* (mister). It is a way of indicating that a boy is not acting as manfully as he might. The *gyaru otoko* is a "girl man," a man who has girlish mannerisms, and the *gyaru oyaji*, or "girl dad," is the middle-aged man who comports himself in a girlish manner.

H

HE. Breaking wind.

This is a straightforward, down-to-earth term, like the English words "fart" and "poot." Unlike its English equivalents, however, *he* has a reputable literary background. It is related to the formal word *hōhi*, the expression favored by Japanese authors throughout the ages when they felt the need to mention farts in respectable literary works.

The character *hō* stands for "sending out" (as in *hōsō*, to broadcast), and *hi* signifies "air" or "wind." The indigenous reading of the character *hi* is *he*, which has become one of the most popular terms for fart.*

In everyday usage *hiru*, "to flutter," and *suru*, "to do," are added to make *he* into a verb:

> *Dare ga he o hitta?*
> Who farted?
> *Ima he shitan deshō? Aa! Mō! Kusai jan!*
> You just farted, right! Oh, no! What a stink!

The ever-popular Osaka dialect has donated its own bawdy variations to mainstream Japanese with the verbs *koku*, "to do," *tareru*, "to drop," and *kamasu*, "to stink up."

> *He o koita.*
> He let one rip.

---

* A scandalous haiku by the medieval master poet Sōkan (1464–1552) goes:

Waga oya no	Even as my father
Shinuru toki ni mo	Lay dying
He o kokite	I farted.

61

He o tareta.
He let one go.
He o kamashita.
He cracked a fart.

The Osaka dialect, cherished in Japan for its liveliness, has further contributed fart-related words like *hetare* and *hekoki*, both literally meaning "farter," but generally used to accuse someone of idiocy.

Ano hetare ore no kane nusunda!
That idiot stole my money!
Nanka monku aru no ka? Hekoki!
So what's your problem, idiot?

Related to *he* is the comical word *sukashippe*, which refers to a silent fart. It was created from *sukashi*, "transparent," *pe* used in place of *he* to facilitate pronunciation.

Sukashippe o suru tsumori datta ga, oto dashichatta.
I was gonna fart discreetly, but I really let one rip.
Dōshite mo gaman ga dekinakunatchatte, sukashippe o shichatta!
I just couldn't hold back, so I let one fly!

A type of fart especially popular among small Japanese schoolboys is the *nigirippe*. *Nigiru* means to clasp or to hold tight, and *pe* (from *he*) is fart. The technique involves farting into one's clenched fist and then quickly holding one's hand up to one's friend's nose.

Mattaku ano chibigaki! Ichinichijū nigirippe shite! Komatta!
That nasty little brat! He's been passing farts around all day!
Mata nigirippe shitara, anta no shiri tataku yo!
If I ever see you pull that little fart trick again, I'll spank your bottom!

A synonym for *nigirippe* is *tsukambe*, literally "catching the fart," an expression originating in the Tohoku dialects.

Uchi no otō-san tondemonai yo! Mata tsukambe shite sā!
My dad's so gross! He's constantly passing around farts!
Mō sono toshi ni natte, tsukambe nanka shinaide yo! Ojii-chan!
C'mon, grandpa! Still doing that fart-in-hand trick at your age?

Quite a few popular proverbs use farts as their subject matter. These proverbs are always fun, although one must be careful as to when and where they are used.

He o koite, shiri o subomu.
Having farted, he closed his ass.

This refers to the wrong-doer who, after an indiscretion, assumes a nonchalant air.

Itachi no saigobe.
A weasel's final fart.

This refers to a last desperate action, the belief being that a hunted weasel at the end of its tether will fart into its pursuer's face hoping that the shock will enable it to escape.

He hitotsu wa kusuri sempuku ni mukau.
One fart is worth a thousand pills.

This is the motto of a typical Japanese granny. A loose translation would be "a fart a day keeps the doctor away."

The other word ranking with *he* in popularity is *onara*. *O* is a softening, honorific prefix, and *nara* means "sound," as in *narasu*, "to ring, sound, or blow."

Ōki na onara o shite shimatta!
He really let one rip!
Daiji na kaigichū ni onara shichatta!
He farted right in the middle of an important conference.

HERO. Heroin.

The *hero* or *heroin* that hits the Japanese streets is mainly imported and controlled by the Yakuza through well-established connections with Hong Kong and Thailand. The drug-smugglers, the dealers, the users, and the cliques they associate with have over the years created an exclusive heroin vocabulary rich in synonyms. Special words were created to define its quality and potency, to characterize the different people that come in contact with it, and to name the paraphernalia needed to consume it.

Hero, as a contraction of *heroin*, is a popular slang word everyone understands.

> *Hero o utsu.*
> To shoot up heroin.
> *Hero o kagu.*
> To snort heroin.
> *Hero yatta koto aru?*
> Ever done any heroin?

Drug cliques more than any other group on the edge of society need a private jargon to confuse eavesdropping outsiders. A common trick in Japanese slang is the inversion of words in order to make them incomprehensible. As *hero* was never much of a secret, *rohe* often took its place.

> *Kon'ya rohe o shiireyō ze!*
> Let's go shopping for some dope tonight!
> *Hayaku rohe o shiirete konakya!*
> I need to get my hands on some dope quickly!

Following international trends in drug lingo, the next logical degree of contraction after *hero* would be H (pronounced *eichi*) or *he*. This proved difficult in Japan, as the popular slang term for "pervert," turned out to be a tough hurdle, with the result that only a few stalwart Westernized drug cliques in

Japan use *H* or *eichi* to refer to heroin. As *he* is equally inappropriate—it means "fart"—the final consensus on Japanese streets settled on *pe* as the preferred clandestine form.

> *Sukoshi pe o yarō ze!*
> C'mon, let's do some H!
> *Ken mata pe sū?*
> Ken's smoking H again?

Two synonyms for heroin that are also frequently inverted are *kona*, "flour," which can become *nako*, and *tane*, "seed," which can become *neta*.

> *Ano kona doko de te ni ireta no?*
> Where did you get hold of that snow?
> *Nako ichikiro mitsuyunyū shita.*
> I smuggled in a kilo of stuff.
> *Sono neta to hoka no mon' mikkusu shinē hō ga mi no tame da ze! Oboeteru darō, Ken no koto?*
> Don't mix this H with other stuff! Remember what happened to Ken?
> *Omē tane sutte'ru no ka yo?? Utta hō ga yoppodo kikun da ze!*
> You smoke this stuff?? You get more outa shooting it up!

High quality *neta* can be referred to as *mabuneta*, "shining seed," or in specific reference to heroin *nambā yon*, "number four," (the standard term on international drug markets to specify the highest quality Hong Kong heroin).

> *Oi! Kore sugē mabuneta ja nē ka! Ore . . . mō . . . mero mero!*
> Man! This stuff's awesome! Wow! I'm really fucked up!
> *Ore ga sabaite'ru no wa nambā yon dake da ze!*
> I only sell number four stuff!

A new fashion on the street for measuring heroin is to refer to the usual one-gram quantity as *G*, pronounced *jii*; anything beyond that is counted in the usual form: *ni guramu*, "two grams," *san guramu*, "three grams."

HERO

> *Hero jii katta yo.*
> I bought a gram of "aitch."
> *Ima pe ni guramu ikura?*
> How much is two grams of H now?

The favorite indirect reference to heroin is *butsu*, "thing"; other fashionable euphemisms are *shiro*, "white"; *matsu*, "powder"; *fummatsu*, "flour"; and *yuki*, "snow," all of which can also be used to refer to cocaine or other white, powdery drugs.

> *Kono butsu hitofukuro sabakitai.*
> I wanna sell this bag of stuff.
> *Dare ka shiro utte'ru?*
> Anyone selling H?
> *Ki o tsukero! Ano matsu dame da!*
> Be careful, man! This sugar's bogus!
> *Ano fummatsu ima yaru?*
> You gonna do this powder now?
> *Kinō no yuki warukatta! Honto ni byōki ni natchatta!*
> That snow yesterday was bad! I really got sick!

Along with other hard drugs, heroin is often referred to as *kusuri*, "medicine," or in its inverted form, *sukuri*.

> *Omē ki o tsuketa hō ga ii ze! Kono kusuri saiaku da!*
> You'd better be careful! This stuff's bogus!
> *Kono sukuri sugē usumete atte! Zenzen kikanē jan!*
> This stuff's too diluted! I don't feel shit!

Other inversions of *kusuri*, popular because they also act as puns, are *risuku*, "risk," *kurisu*, "Chris," and *suriku*, "slick."

> *Sono supūn yokose yo! Risuku no jikan da!*
> Hand me the spoon! It's time to fix the stuff!
> *Ano kurisu ippatsu de buttonda ze! Ore nanka hikari ni tsutsumarete shimatta ze!*
> One shot of this and I was flying! I was really tripping!*

---

* Literally, "I was covered with lights."

66

Omae sonna boroi chūshaki de suriku utsu ki ka yo!
You're not gonna shoot up with that fucked-up needle, are you?

HEROCHŪ. Heroin addict.

The correct term for "heroin addict" is *heroin chūdoku kanja*, a cumbersome mouthful avoided on the streets in favor of shorter, slangier expressions.

In the twenties, the word *aruchū*, for alcoholic, appeared on the Japanese scene (from *arukōru chūdoku*, or "alcohol addiction"). When heroin usage increased, this term inspired the word *herochū*, a contraction of *heroin chūdoku*, "addicted to heroin," which has remained one of the most popular slang terms for the heroin addict.

> *Ano herochū no ude wa akai hanten darake.*
> That smackslammer's arm is full of red marks.
> *Ken wa herochū? Shiranakatta!*
> Ken's a dope-head? I didn't know that!

Two popular words for "junkie" in Japan's drug world are *herokan* (from *heroin kanja*, "heroin patient") and the closely related *pekan*, from the same term.

> *Ore no dachi wa minna herokan dakara.*
> My friends are all a bunch of junkies.
> *Kono manshon wa pekan-tachi darake!*
> This building is full of heroin addicts!

Other favorites for "heroin junkie" are *pechū*, from *heroin chūdoku* (addicted to heroin), and *peboke*, from *pe* (heroin) and *boke* (from *bokeru*, "to be muddled")

> *Kono butsu o pechū no dachi kara te ni ireta.*
> I got this stuff from a junkie friend of mine.
> *Ano peboke bāsan no koto mo uri ni dashikanenē!*
> That junkie would sell his own grandmother!

HAMERU

Japanese anti-drug laws are very harsh. Heroin addicts are much more careful than their American peers about where they buy the drug and where they consume it. Special apartments or "pads" where heroin can be bought and used in a safe environment are known as *hero kutsu* or *pe kutsu, kutsu* being short for *dōkutsu*, or "cavern."

> *Ore sugē ii herokutsu shitte'ru kara, itte yarō ze!*
> I know a good pad where we can go and shoot up!
> *Na! Ima sugu yo! Pe kutsu ikō ze! Ore, yo! Ima, yo! Hitouchi hitsuyō nan da yo!*
> Man, hurry up! Quick, let's go to the den! Man, I need a fix, man!

HAMERU. To put in.

Hameru belongs to a group of words that should be used with caution as they have strong sexual undertones. *Botan o hamenasai!* (Do your buttons up!) or *tebukuro o hamenasai!* (Wear your gloves!) are everyday idiomatic expressions. The danger lies in that *hamenasai!* can just as well be interpreted to mean "Stick it in me!" or "Give it to me!"

> *Hamete chōdai!*
> Fuck me!
> *Hajimete dendokokeshi o hamete mitara, sugokatta!*
> When I stuck a vibrator in for the first time, it was great.

To create a slightly stronger synonym, *komu*, which suggests entering with force, can be added to *hameru*, creating *hamekomu*.

> *Fukaku hamekonde chōdai!*
> Ram it in deep!
> *Nē! Anta hamekomu toki, mō chotto yasashiku shite kuretara ii no ni!*
> I wish you'd be a bit gentler when you stick it in!

Another technical but risky word for insertion is *sōnyū*. Handle with care, as it is stronger than hameru or hamekomu. Its two characters are *sō*, meaning "put in," and *nyū* meaning "enter." Although it appears in every dictionary, its sexual undertones have become too strong for it to be safely used in public.

> *Tampon o sōnyū suru.*
> To insert a tampon.
> *Kare ga gin gin no sōnyū shite kita!*
> He inserted his pulsating meat!

The next rung down on the ladder of roughness brings us to *tsukkomu*, which literally means "to thrust into" or "to plunge into" (the character *tsuku* meaning "to stab," and *komu* meaning "into").

Tsukkomu can be used in everyday speech in combinations like *"poketto ni te o tsukkonda"* (he thrust his hands into his pockets), but be advised that the average Japanese will make an immediate association with sexual thrusting.

> *Chimpo o tsukkonda.*
> He thrust his dick in.
> *Kanojo no kuchi ni tsukkonjatta!*
> He thrust it into her mouth!

To add even more force to *tsuku*, the suffix *makuru* (over and over), which originated in the dialects of the Kansai region but is now popular all over Japan, is often added, creating *tsukimakuru*, "to stab again and again."

> *Anta! Itsumade mo tsukimakutte!*
> Baby! Keep shoving it in forever!
> *Doa ga aita toki, ore kanojo no ana ni tsukimakutte'ta!*
> I was hammering away at her when the door opened!

The harshest of these six technical terms is *bukkomu*. The character for this word is *butsu*, meaning to "hit," and *komu* meaning "into."

Fukaku oku made bukkonde!
Ram it in all the way!
Atashi kare ga ikisō ni naru no wakarun da yo nē! Sugē ikioi de bukkomu kara sā!
I can always tell when he's about to come 'cause he starts humping away like crazy!

HAKO. Vagina.

Many of the in-vogue terms for vagina in the darker alleys of the Japanese street scene are words depicting it as a receptacle.

Hako, "box," together with restaurant utensils like pots, plates, jugs, beakers, and the all-important sakè cups, constitute a substantial segment of the taboo terms that were created after dark when the boys got together for drinks and a bit of conversation.

Ato, hako yari ni ikō ka?
You wanna get us some pussy after this?
Atarashii sutorippā no hako mita? Sugē!
Did you see the new stripper's box? Hot!

After a hard day at work it is customary for male workers in Japan to hit the scene, while wives and girlfriends stay at home. The relaxed and predominantly masculine tone of such "boys on the town" outings often inspires intimate discussions that become franker as the men become more sloshed. When these conversations call for either a precise differentiation among vaginas or an accurate description of one, the dishes on the table, the bowls of food, and the sakè cups have all proved excellent analogies for organs of every shape, size, and color.

The *sara* or *ōzara* are large, shallow dishes that can be used to refer to vaginas that are wide but not deep.

Ore don don tsukimakutte, kanojo no sara no kabe made itchimatta.
I pushed my way in deeper and deeper until I hit her sugar-walls.

Suzuko no ōzara wa Roppongi ja saikō da ze!
Suzuko has the best twat in Roppongi!

The vagina of a young girl or virgin can be referred to as *atarabachi,* "new pot," or *ochoko,* "small sakè cup."

Kanojo no atarabachi shimatte'ru!
Her little snatch is real tight!
Omae no ochoko de yarashite kure yo na!
Come let me play with your little pussy!

A vagina that is deep and easily penetrable by a penis can be called *ohachi,* "deep bowl" or *suribachi,* an earthenware mortar.

Ore kanojo no ohachi ni muriyari irekondara, mō tengoku datta ze!
When I plunged deep into her crack, it was heaven!
Washi no onna wa suribachi no tsukaikata o yoku shitte oru!
My woman really knows how to work that love-muscle!

Other receptacles popular as bawdy synonyms for vagina are *utsuwa,* "container," and *meiki,* "vase." *Meiki* is used to specify a top-quality vagina, and has become so popular as a sexual slang word that its original meaning of "vase" has been all but forgotten.

Ore no mono o iretara, kanojo no utsuwa piku piku furuwasete'ta!
When I put it in, her cunt started quivering!
Omae kanojo no meiki ni yubi o tsukkonda'tte? Temē na!
You put your finger up her snatch! You dog!

HIMO. Pimp.

A procurer is formally known in Japanese as a *baishun assen gyōsha* (literally, prostitute-mediator-tradesman). Not an easy word to get one's tongue around, which is why on the streets and in everyday speech the preferred expression is *himo. Himo* literally means "string" or "rope," the idea being that pimps "rope" the girls in and "tie" them to their work.

This term dates back to the days of the *aosen*, "blue-line," and *akasen*, "red-line" districts, before prostitution was made illegal in 1958. The blue-line district was the officially designated area of town where licensed prostitutes and their pimps could legally work, while the red-line district housed the unlicensed girls.

> *Tokyo de himo no seikatsu o shite'ru.*
> He's working as a pimp in Tokyo.
> *Ore Ken ga himo da nante, shiranakatta ze! Yaru jan!*
> I didn't know Ken was a pimp! Wild !

A prostitute who works for a pimp is known on the streets as *himotsuki*, "pimp-attached," or the Osaka slang version that is now heard a lot, *hibotsuki*.

> *Kono bā no onna wa minna himotsuki.*
> All the girls in this bar work with pimps.
> *Suzuko hibotsuki dakedo, hoka demo shigoto o shite'ru.*
> Suzuko has a pimp, but she does a bit of work on the side.

It has recently become fashionable for yuppie Tokyo girls who support their poor student boyfriends to refer to them playfully as *himo*.

> *Atashi no himo ga ne! Motto kane kure'tte iu no yo ne!*
> You know that guy of mine! He wants more money again!
> *Atashi no ima made no himo'tte, ii kao wa shite'n da yo nē, minna!*
> All my boyfriends have always been pretty but poor!

In the red-light district, pimps themselves prefer to be called *manējā*, "manager," or *pōtā*, "porter," but do not take kindly to being called *himo*, which is as uncomplimentary as the English "pimp."

Anta no manējā dare?
Who's your dude?
Aitsu Osaka de pōtā yatte, hitomōke shita ze!
He made a bundle working as a pimp in Osaka!

Another popular word for pimp is *pombiki.* As pimping in the traditional sense is illegal in Japan today, the modern *pombiki* stands outside different red-light establishments trying to boost his income by luring in as many customers as possible. (He gets paid *per capita.*)

Pombiki de ikura ni naru ka na?
I wonder how much a pimp makes here?
Kono hen no pombiki'tte honto ni shitsukoi ze! Hipparikomō to suru mon na!
The macks around here are so pushy! They like pull you off the street!

The English-inspired equivalent to *pombiki* is *kyatchiman* (the catch-man).

Atarashii kyatchiman dō ka ne? Tsukaeru ka ne?
How's the new dude we hired? Any use?
Shitsukoi kyatchiman ni wa ki o tsukero yo.
Be careful of the pushy pimps.

A recent arrival on the slang scene is a comical word for pimp that was inspired by Shakespeare's *Merchant of Venice.* *Benisu,* "Venice," was slightly altered to create *penisu,* "penis," resulting in *penisu no shōnin,* "the merchant of penis," i.e., the pimp.

Kono hen penisu no shōnin ga kane o kassegimakutte'ru!
Man! The pimps in this area must really be raking in the money!
Omē koko de nani yatte'n da yo? Penisu no shōnin ka?
What are you doing around here? You selling women or something?

HIROPON. Amphetamine.

The biggest drug problem in Japan today is the abuse of amphetamines. The situation is so disastrous that drug-abuse specialists have labeled Tokyo the speed capital of the world! It all started just over a hundred years ago, in 1887, when the first amphetamine was invented. There was dancing in the streets. The 1880s were the decade of miracle drugs. First heroin (a name inspired by the word "heroic"; it was thought at the time to be a miraculous elixir of life and inspiration), and then the amphetamines, which promised limitless supplies of energy coupled with self-confidence and euphoria. This wonder drug soon reached the laboratories of the Western-trained scientists of Meiji-period Japan. Within five years a Japanese doctor had created his own amphetamine compound, *philopon* (pronounced *hiropon*), which had a marvelous effect on his manic-depressive patients.

The first mass-production of amphetamines (in Japan and in the West) came forty years later during World War II, when tons of the stuff were given to soldiers all over the world to dull their hunger, keep them as euphoric as possible, and provide prolonged bursts of energy.

Japan's drug problem started in 1945, when the Japanese soldiers, the Japanese amphetamine factories, and the American servicemen dropped their surplus amphetamines on the market. By 1953 there were over half a million addicts. In 1954 the Japanese government passed its first anti-amphetamine laws. While Western amphetaminists "pop" the drug in pill form, the Japanese inject it.

> *Hiropon o utsu.*
> To shoot-up amphetamines.
> *Kare no ude wa hiropon de fukureagatte'ru.*
> His arm's really fucked up from all those speed injections.

The official media word for amphetamine is *kakuseizai*, "awakening medicine," while the word used on the street is the actual brand-name *hiropon*, in drug circles just *pon*.

> *Aitsu-ra kakuseizai mitsuyu de taiho sareta.*
> They got arrested for smuggling in speed.
> *Pon ippon utsu no ikura?*
> How much is a shot of speed?

The tons of *hiropon* that hit Japan's streets today are manufactured in illicit Yakuza-run factories, many of which are in South Korea and, lately, the Philippines. Once the drugs are smuggled into Japan they are sold on the streets by the *pombai*, the amphetamine dealers.

> *Omae ni ii pombai shōkai shite yaru ze!*
> I'll introduce you to a cool speed dealer!
> *Kono hen no atarashii pombai dare da? Ken ka?*
> Who's the new speed dealer around here? Ken?

The amphetamine junkie, whether teacher, housewife, student, or factory worker, is known on Japan's streets as *ponchū* (from *hiropon chūdoku*, amphetamine-addicted). Collectively they are called *ponchū zoku*, "the amphetamine-addict gang."

> *Oi! Ano ponchū shinisō ja nē ka!*
> Man, that A-freak looks like he's dying!
> *Ano ponchū mikka nete nē no ni, mada gin gin da ze!*
> That A-freak ain't slept for three days, and he's still goin' strong!

The present Amphetamine Control Law calls for seven years to life in prison for amphetamine dealing. (In 1987 there were 20,966 arrests, according to the *Japan Journal*). Illicit safehouses or "amp pads," known as *ponkutsu*, "amphetamine caverns," have sprung up nationwide. Here addicts buy, sell, and indulge their addiction in a friendly and relatively safe club-like atmosphere.

Omē no ponkutsu, ikura gurai da yo?
What are the prices like at your A-pad?
Moto yaoya datta no o aitsu-ra ponkutsu ni shita!
It used to be a grocery, but they turned it into an A-pad!

HOMMEI-KUN. Mr. Favorite.

Mr. Favorite arrived on the slang scene at the beginning of the nineties as one of five words that differentiate the types of boyfriend really trendy Japanese girls keep at their beck and call.

In the hierarchy of boyfriend-importance Mr. Favorite, or *Hommei-kun*, has managed to clinch the top position; *Kiipu-kun* is a close second, followed by *Mitsugu-kun, Ashi-kun,* and last and least, *Benri-kun.*

Ima hommei-kun kara denwa atta no. Yappari, aishite'ru'tte!
My main man just called me on the phone. He loves me after all!
Kondo no dōnichi atashi dare ni denwa shiyō ka nā! Hommei-kun Osaka e itchaun da yo nee!
Who shall I call this weekend? My main squeeze's gonna be in Osaka!

Kiipu-kun, Mr. Keep, is a boyfriend kept within call by the prudent girl just in case something happens to Mr. Favorite.

Kenji wa kyō isogashii kara, Kiipu-kun ni denwa shite miyō.
Kenji's busy tonight, so I'm gonna call my stand-by.
Sonna ni naigashiro ni shitcha dame yo! Kiipu-kun motte'te son wa nain da kara!
Don't be so nasty to him! Just keep him as a backup!

The next runner-up, *Mitsugu-kun*, Mr. Supply, wines, dines, and "supplies" the young socialite with a shower of presents, but other than an occasional smile or encouraging word he can't expect much unless something unforeseen happens to Mr. Favorite and Mr. Keep.

76

*Kondo no Mitsugu-kun wa mashi yo ne! Kao wa warui kedo
kanemochi da shi!*
This sugar daddy's better than the last one! He might
look like shit but he's loaded!
Mite! Mite! Mitsugu-kun ga katte kureta no kawaii deshō?
Look, look what my sugar daddy bought me! Ain't it
cute?

Next in line is *Ashi-kun*, Mr. Leg, also called *ashi*, "leg," for
short. The main prerequisite for becoming an *Ashi-kun* is to
have a car and be available around the clock to drive the young
girl around. Being the girl's "leg" in this sense is the only
privilege an *Ashi-kun* can ever hope to attain.

Nē! Anta no ashi ni denwa shite! Kon'ya dok'ka dekakeyō yo!
Call that guy you know with the car! Let's go out tonight!
*Anta no ashi no kuruma no hō ga kakkoii kara, denwa shite
kurenai?*
Your car-friend's car's cooler than mine! Give him a call,
OK?

Coming in last is *Benri-kun*, Mr. Useful. Without car, money,
or looks worth mentioning, he qualifies for the menial jobs
(plumbing repairs, grocery shopping, and the like).

*Masaka! Atashi kare to nanka nenai yo! Tada no Benri-kun da
mon!*
Come on! I don't sleep with him! He's just someone
useful to have around!
*Kanojo ga ore no koto Benri-kun ni shiyō to shite'run dattara
gomen da ze!*
If she thinks I'm just gonna be some idiot she can use,
forget it!

Two unfortunate boyfriends who do not even make the
above five categories are the *hoken otoko*, and the *nichi*. The *hoken*
(insurance) *otoko* (man) comes into the picture only as an
absolute last resort when a desperate girl is stuck.

Ken wa honto ni hoken otoko da kara itsudemo tayori ni naru no yo!
Ken's a great backup boyfriend, I can always rely on him!

The plight of the *nichi* is no better. As its etymology suggests (it is a fusion of the words *nii-chan*, meaning "elder brother," and *ashi* meaning "leg," or in this case "driver"), not only must the poor *nichi* play the role of driver, but in addition can expect no more than a curt sisterly thank you for his troubles.

Nichi wa atashi no tame ni jibun de shinsha katta no yo! Kawaii no!
That little boy bought a brand new car to impress me! Ain't that cute!

The plight of the boyfriend, as Japan enters the twenty-first century, has reached a hysterical pitch that has engendered the unprecedented *hosuto genshō*, the "gigolo phenomenon." Here the traditional Japanese boy-girl roles are reversed. The hapless young man is so eager to please his date that he fawns on her as only a well-trained gigolo would. He tells amusing little stories to keep her entertained, opens doors to let her go first, pours beer for her and then quickly pours his own before she can return the favor, and in general will do any number of small gentlemanly things that would lead a Japanese girl who was not trendy to doubt his sanity.

I

ICHIMON NASHI. Penniless.

This popular expression dates back to Edo times, when the *mon* was a little brass coin with a hole in it, equivalent to a modern penny. Although the *mon* is long gone, the slang expression *ichimon nashi*, or *mon*-less, is as popular as ever.

> *Aitsu ichimon nashi!*
> He's cleaned out!
> *Ore nanka mō, ichimon nashi da ze!*
> Man! I'm like flat broke!

In rougher street circles the related expression *hai nashi* is favored. Similar to *mon*, *hai*, standing for "one yen," was the lowest unit of currency after the *mon* went out of circulation.

> *Kanojo wa kane o zembu nusumarete, hai nashi ni natta!*
> She was cleaned out! They snatched all her money!
> *Kanojo wa otoko ni mitsugu kara, hai nashi nan da.*
> She works for this guy, so she's always broke.

When someone becomes penniless in gambling circles the applicable expression is *yari nashi*. This term uses the sub-rosa gambling slang word for "one," which is *yari*. In secret gambling get-togethers, the numbers one through ten are: *yari* (1), *furi* (2), *kara* (3), *tame* (4), *zuka* (5), *mizu* (6), *oki* (7), *ata* (8), *gake* (9), and *chiki* (10).

> *Ore yari nashi da! Ichiman en kashite kure!*
> I'm broke, man! Lend me ten thousand yen!

Anta hanafuda yamete kurenai? Dōse yari nashi de owarun dakara sa!
I wish you'd stop gambling! You always end up penniless!

The person who is *ichimon nashi, hai nashi,* or *yari nashi* can be classified in fashionable street slang as a *hinkuya*. This humorous but unflattering expression is made up of the three characters *hin,* meaning "poor," *ku,* "worry," and *ya,* "person."

Ano aware na hinkuya nanka ni, kane yarun ja nai yo!
Don't give that bum any cash!
Hinkuya dakara piza hitotsu mo kaenai yo!
I'm so broke I can't even afford a slice of pizza!

In order to extend *hinkuya's* range, innovative slang users change it into an adjective by adding the suffixes *-ppoi* or *-mitai,* and into a verb by adding *yaru.*

Aitsu wa sugē kanemochi dakedo, kao ga hinkuya-ppoi zo!
Though that guy's real rich he looks like a bum!
Kono bā wa hinkuya-mitai na yatsu darake!
This bar's teeming with bums!
Tokyo ni isshūkan mo ittara hinkuyatta.
One week in Tokyo and I was cleaned out.

Another handy noun used in the shadier parts of town to single out a person on the ropes is *okera,* "mole cricket," or *okera otoko,* "mole-cricket man," or *okera onna,* "mole-cricket woman."

Omae shinjirarenai hayasa de okera ni natchimatta yo na!
Man you really went broke fast!
Anna boroguruma ni notte, minna omae o okera otoko to omou!
If you drive around in a wreck like this people will think you're some kinda bum!
Sonna no kite'tara okera onna mitai!
You look like a bag lady in that dress!

Two general slang words for destitution are the melodious *sukkarakan*, an Osaka dialect importation, and the newer concoction *kinketsubyō*. *Sukkarakan* was originally written with two characters, *su*, "basis" or "foundation," and *kara*, "empty." *Kinketsubyō* is written with three characters, *kin* for "gold" or "money," *ketsu* meaning "lacking," and *byō*, "illness," literally "the no-money sickness."

> *Ima sukkarakan dakara kongetsu no yachin ga haraenain da yo na.*
> I'm so broke I can't pay the rent this month.
> *Ore no kinketsubyō wa gyamburu no sei da!*
> I'm so broke 'cause of gambling!

A recent arrival on the slang scene is *mikuro seikatsu*, "microlife," which is used by students to describe the debilitating hardships of a moneyless existence.

> *Ore Tokyo ni kite kara mikuro seikatsu da ze!*
> Ever since I've come to Tokyo I've been livin' on the ragged edge!
> *Kanojo itsumo mikuro seikatsu no koto monku itte'ru kedo! Hatarakeba ii ja nai nē!*
> She's always complaining about being dead poor! Why doesn't she just get a job?

The newest and zaniest words for "poor," "poorer," and "poorest" sprang from the ever-groovy Tokyo high school scene; it is a wordplay on *bimbō* (poor), that relies on the English comparatives, which yields *bimbō*, "poor," *bimb*-er (pronounced *bimbā*), "poorer," and *bimb*-est (pronounced *bimbesuto*) "poorest."

> *Atashi no kare kyonen bimbō datta to suru to, kotoshi wa bimbā da yo!*
> If my boyfriend was dirt poor last year, this year he's even dirt poorer!

Ore baito sagasō! Kurasu de bimbesuto na no wa iya da!
I have to find some part-time work! I hate being the piss-poorest in class!

IMAICHI. Not up to par.

Since the early eighties this expression has gained a strong foothold in Japanese slang. *Imaichi* was made up of *ima hitotsu taranai*, meaning "one thing is missing at this point," the implication being that something important, possibly the most important thing, is missing. Something or someone *imaichi* is deficient. In American slang *imaichi* is comparable to "crappy" "doesn't hack it," or even "half-assed."

> *Aitsu imaichi.*
> He's a loser.
> *Koko no kōhii imaichi da yo!*
> The coffee in this place is crappy!

To reinforce a statement of disapproval, *imani* or *imasan* can be used. *Imani* implies that at least two things are missing, and *imasan* even three. In school slang this progression is taken by high schoolers partial to hyperbole into the two- and three-digit numbers, engendering words like *imahyaku* (now a hundred things are missing), *imasen* (now a thousand things are missing) and the mind-boggling *imajūman* (now a hundred thousand things are missing). These formulations, emphatic though they may be, are frowned upon by more mature users of slang.

> *Omae-ra imani!*
> You guys are such jerks!
> *Kono dōbutsuen imahyaku!*
> This school (zoo) is totally gross!
> *Ano kuso senko koroshite yaru! Aitsu imajūman!*
> I'm gonna kill that asshole teacher! He's the fuckin' pits!

Another popular way of defining something or someone as "gross," "pukey," or in general nauseating beyond description is by using *gero gero*. This onomatopoeic expression originated in Osaka slang, where the word *gero* means "vomit." *Gero gero*, literally "vomity," can be used by itself or as an adjective with the particle *na*.

> *Kono kuso gakkō gero gero!*
> This fuckin' school grosses me out!
> *Nan da kono gero gero na doresu!*
> What's with this shitty dress you're wearing!

IMO. Hick.

For generations *imo*, the potato, has been a symbol of the hick in Japan. Any Japanese not born or at least raised in Tokyo or in another of the metropolises could qualify in urban slang as an *imo*.

In the past decade the potato, in its scorn of out-of-towners, has acquired new dimensions.

> *Gee! Ano imo sugē kakkō shite'ru!*
> Man! I can't believe what that hick's wearing!
> *Nani shabette'n no ka waka'nnai yo, ano imo!*
> I don't understand a word this bumpkin's saying!

Even more offensive than *imo* is *imo yarō*, "potato guy."

> *Ano imo yarō jibun no koto kakkoii to omotte'n no! Tondemonē!*
> This geek thinks he's cool! Well, I got news for him!

To be cruel to out-of-town girls *imo nē-chan*, "potato sister," was invented.

> *Ore warui kedo! Anna imo nē-chan to dēto shinē yo!*
> Sorry, man! No way I'm gonna go on a date with a yokel like her!

In the past decade, new generations have improvised on the motif of the potato as a symbol of provinciality, creating a whole new line of potato-related insults. *Imobēda*, fusing *imo* with the English word "invader" (from the video game "space invaders") originated in the Tokyo video arcades in the late 1980s.

> *Kono disuko ni ku'n no wa imobēda dake da yo!*
> The only people goin' to this club are hillbillies!
> *Chikayo'nnai de yo! Kono imobēda!*
> Get away from me, you hick!

Potato terms originating in Tokyo's schools are *potēto* itself and *imozoku*, "potato gang."

> *Ano potēto ota ota ota ota shichatte, shōganai na! Tokyo ni narete nai kara na!*
> I'm not surprised that poor hick's freaking out! He's not used to Tokyo!
> *Ore Tokyo ni kaeritē yo! Kono hen no yatsu-ra minna imozoku nan da mon!*
> I wanna go back to Tokyo! This dump's fulla hicks!

The newest imo-related insults on the slang scene are potato croquettes, *korokke*, and potato chips, *imochi* (an abbreviated version of *imo chippusu*).

> *Oi! Korokke! Dok'kara kitan da yo!*
> Man, what a boob! What stone did you crawl out from under?
> *Asoko ni atsumatte'n no wa minna imochi!*
> The dudes who hang out there are a bunch of hicks!

If a person from the provinces is a "potato," a "croquette," or a "chip," then his actions or style could be labeled "potato-esque," "croquette-ish," or "chip-like." The endings *-kusai*, *-ppoi*, and *-chikku* (from the "tic" in romantic) can be added to any of the above nouns to turn them into adjectives such as *imo-kusai, imo-ppoi, imo-chikku,* or *potēto-chikku*.

Aa! Mō! Uchi no okā-san imo-ksai! Issho ni dearukitakunai yo!
God! My mother's such a hick! I can't stand to be seen
with her!

Ano ko no apāto'tte, chō-imo-ppoi!
That girl's apartment's just *so* tacky!

Imo-chikku hanasanaide yo! Kikoeru ja nai!
Don't talk like a hillbilly! People will hear!

*Atashi kare to disuko ni itte mo, potēto-chikku odoru kara 'ya
na no!*
I don't wanna be seen in a club with him! He dances like
some hick!

J

JORŌ. Prostitute.

This is one of the favorite words for prostitute among a group of terms that originated as early Edo-period slang (1600–1867). They have not lost their popularity over the centuries. The character *jo* means woman, and *rō* is a masculine name ending.

> *Ano jorō-me!*
> That slut!
> *Aitsu wa jorō o yatte, kane o takusan mōketan da ze!*
> She made a bundle as a whore!

Two anti-*jorō* proverbs popular with street-wise grannies all over Japan are:

> *Jorō no makoto to tamago no shikaku.*
> A whore is as honest as an egg is square.
> *Jorōgai no hiyameshi.*
> He who buys whores eats cold rice.
> (The message being that he who wastes all his money in the red-light district will be financially ruined.)

Another favorite slang word dating back to Edo times is *abazure*. It is made up of *aba*, a word of Chinese origin meaning "old woman," and *zure*, an indigenous Japanese word for "cheeky" or "saucy." What was originally a saucy old woman has come to mean in modern times a loud-mouthed slut.

> *Abazure onna mitai!*
> She looks like a slut!

Ki o tsukero yo na! Ano onna abazure dakara na!
Careful, man! That woman's bad news!

Another Edo-period red-light district word that has survived the ravages of time is *baita*. *Baita* means "prostitute," and is made up of the characters *bai*, meaning "sale," and *ta*, meaning "woman." When used today, it gives a statement an arch but nasty flavor.

Baita no seikatsu nante korigori!
I've had enough of this whore's life!
Kono atari wa baita no kasegidokoro yo!
The whores rake in the cash in this neighborhood!

Like all the other fashionable but venerable words, *baita* has its entourage of quotable proverbs.

Baita no soranaki.
The crocodile tears of a prostitute.
Baita ni makoto nashi.
Never trust a whore.

K

KECHI. Stingy.

Kechi originated during the early Edo period. It was initially pronounced *keshi* and meant "shabby" or "dingy." Over time this term grew in currency, reaching full dictionary respectability during the Showa period. Recent linguistic trends have given *kechi* a feminine touch; many men avoiding it as being too cute.

> *Onegai otō-san! Kechi!*
> Oh come on, dad! You're so stingy!
> *Kanojo wa kechi dakara zenzen asobi ni dekakenai!*
> She's so stingy she never goes anywhere!

To emphasize someone's tight-fistedness you can use *kechi* twice or add the popular Osaka-dialect *do-*.

> *Kechi kechi shinaide!*
> Don't be so stingy!
> *Do-kechi dakara mō issho ni dekakenai!*
> He's so tight-fisted I'm not going out with him anymore!

Other variations on *kechi* are *kechi-kusai* (looking or acting stingy) or *kechimbō*, "cheapskate" or "tightwad."

> *Dōshite sonna ni kechi-kusai?*
> Why're you so cheap?
> *Ano kechimbō no jiji nani ittan da?*
> What did that old cheapskate tell you?

A stronger, more masculine variation on parsimony is *gametsui*, an expression popular in the Osaka dialect. One of the more entertaining etymologies for *gametsui* is provided by Iguchi Tatsuo in *Shiranai Nihongo-5* (Unknown Japanese-5), where he suggests it is inspired by *kame*, "turtle," and *tsui*, from *tsuku*, "to cling" (the idea being that turtles stubbornly cling on to whatever they bite).

> *Ano gametsui onna-me ore ni kane kaese'tte iiyagaru!*
> That cheap bitch told me to give her her money back!
> *Nan de sonna ni gametsuin da yo?*
> Why are you such a cheapskate?

To emphasize greed and the element of hoarding you can use *gatsu gatsu*. (For maximum effect use *gatsu gatsu gatsu gatsu* in quick succession).

> *Kanojo wa itsumo ie ni ite, gatsu gatsu kane o tamete'ru.*
> She's always home hoarding her money.
> *Uchi no bā-san nannen mo gatsu gatsu gatsu gatsu takuwaete'ru kara ima ja okuman chōja da yo!*
> Grandma's been hoarding cash for years now! She must be a multimillionaire by now!

KEIMUSHO. Prison.

During the 1980s and into the 90s the number of serious crimes in Japan, low to start with, has been on the decline. For those who do transgress, there are currently some seventy-four *keimusho* (prisons) ready and waiting. The word *keimusho* is made up of the three characters *kei*, "punishment," *mu*, "duty," and *sho*, "place." It became the official word for prison at the end of the Taisho period (1912–26), replacing the older *kangoku* (*kan*, "supervise," plus *goku*, "jail"). Today both words are fashionable in the media as well as on the streets.

> *Ore wa Abashiri ni itta ze! Asoko wa sekai ichi hidē keimusho da!*
> I was in Abashiri! Man, the worst prison in the world!

Omae dore gurai kangoku ni ittan da?
How long were you in the pen for?

Also popular are the detention houses, known as *kōchisho*, of which there are over a hundred and twenty nationwide.

Aitsu ga kōchisho ni iku no wa hajimete ja nai kara nā!
It's not the first time he's been locked up!

Imprisonment or confinement is officially called *kankin*, the character *kan* meaning "supervision," and *kin*, "prohibition." Some useful phrases to remember are:

Kankin suru.   To imprison.
Kankin sareru.   To be put in prison.
Kankin saseru.   To get someone put in prison.

Even though *kankin* is the official word for incarceration, it is as familiar in the streets as in the courtroom.

Damare! Omae ore ga kankin sarete mō ii no ka yo?
Shut up! You wanna get me arrested?
Ore hayaku koko denakya! Kankin sarechimau yo!
I've to get the hell outa here! They're gonna arrest me!

The first place one lands after getting arrested is the *butabako* (pig-box), which is the lockup at every local police station. A *butabako* is usually a small room with a wooden floor that is shared by up to five or six suspects awaiting arraignment. A popular street slang variation on *butabako* is *ambako*, "dark box," which can be used for both police cells and prison cells.

Aitsu satsu o uchisokonete butabako ni itchimatta.
He shot at a policeman, so they put him in the clink.
Baka yarō! Koko wa ambako da ze! Onsen ryokō* ja nēn da!
Get your ass in gear! This is a hoosegow, not the Club Med!

---

* Literally, a "hot-spring trip."

One of the more popular words for jail, limited to rough street speech, is *musho*, the last two syllables of *keimusho*.

> *Kawaisō ni, anta no danna mata musho iki datte sā.*
> Your poor old man! So he's inside again.
> *Mata aitsu-ra ga kore no koto kagitsuketara, ore mata musho iki darō na!*
> If they find me with this stuff on me I'll end up in the clink again!

Two tongue-in-cheek street euphemisms for jail are *hoteru*, "hotel," and its inversion *teruho*.

> *Uchi no teishu sengetsu mata hoteru ni haitchatta!*
> My old man's in the Crossbar Hotel again!
> *Ato ichinen de teruho kara derareru!*
> I'm gonna be outa this resort in a year!

Entering prison is unofficially known as *inkyo*, "retiring." The "time" or the "term" that a prisoner serves is colloquially known as *otsutome*, "duty," especially in Yakuza circles, where it is seen as the "duty" of subordinates to do prison terms in place of their bosses.

> *Ore no tsuma mata inkyo shita.*
> My old woman's inside again.
> *Aitsu otsutomechū!*
> He's serving time!

For the Japanese inmate the most important word, the word that gives him hope, the light at the end of the dark tunnel, is *shaba*, "the outside world." *Shaba* originated in India as the Sanskrit *saha*, meaning "the world we live in." It came to Japan in the sixth century B.C. with the advent of Buddhism, and over the centuries has been absorbed into colloquial speech in such expressions as *Mō shaba ni yō wa nai!* (I have no more use for this world).

So while in standard Japanese *shaba* means "this world," "the world we live in," its newer and slangier spin indicates the outside world as opposed to prison life.

Shaba e deru.
To leave prison.
Shaba ni dete koreta kimochi wa dō da?
How does it feel now that you're out?

Inmates impatient to get their share of *shaba* before they are legally eligible might consider what is known in slang as *yaburu*, breaking jail, or *retsuwaru*, a criminal-jargon word for breaking jail with an accomplice *(retsu* is the inversion of *tsure*, "together," and *waru* means "break").

Ore wa yaburu keikaku ga aru.
I've got a plan to get outa here.
Ore-tachi ni wa retsuwaru shika nēn da!
We're gonna have to beat this joint!

KETSU. Ass.

The *proper* word for "posterior" in Japanese is *dembu*, but like its English equivalent its popularity rating in street slang is excessively low. In situations where Americans say "bottom" or "ass," the Japanese words to use are *shiri* or the slightly rougher *ketsu.**

Unko o shita ato ketsu o fuku.
You wipe your ass after you shit.
Kondo watashi ga hirotta otoko wa ōki na kebukai ketsu no otoko yo!
The guy I picked up the other day was big and hairy-assed!

Ketsu is written with the same character as *ana*, which means "hole." The etymology of both *ketsu* and *ana* are hotly argued, especially by some of Japan's more eccentric linguists. Taka

---

* In dialects ranging from Tokyo, Nagoya, Chiba, Gifu, Niigata, and Tokushima, *ketsu* is nowadays also used to as a vulgar slang word for "end" or "last."

Hōryū, for instance, in his popular but idiosyncratic book *Kotoba no Yūrai*, offers the fantastic theory that *ketsu* evolved from *ki*, "life energy," and *tsunageru*, "to connect," the far-fetched idea being that *ketsu* originally meant the whole hip area and was thus the place that two people "connected" in marriage to create "life."

The views on *ana*'s provenance are even more extravagant. One extreme theory proposes that it is of New Zealand origin (*ana* happens to mean "hole" in Maori); another theory even goes so far as to suggest that the Latin word *anus* somehow made the arduous trip from ancient Rome to the shores of Japan, where the primitive people of the Yayoi period (200 B.C. to A.D. 250) turned it into *ana*.

To specify the "anus," *ketsu no ana*, or "asshole," is used:

> *Ketsu no ana de yatta koto aru?*
> You ever fucked anyone up the ass?
> *Ketsu no ana no chiisai yarō!*
> You cheap asshole! (Literally, "Your asshole is small!")

The other important word for ass is *shiri*, "bottom." *Shiri* is softer than *ketsu*, which makes it the preferred word among women.

> *Kono kuriimu shiri ni nureba yoku narimasu.*
> If you rub this cream on your bottom, it'll get better.
> *Omae no shiri kusai!*
> Your ass stinks!

Well-bred girls who find themselves pressured to discuss bottoms in public will usually opt to add the softening honorific prefix *o*.

> *Kare minna no iru mae de atashi no oshiri sawatta no!*
> He grabbed my bottom in front of everyone!

People wishing to use *shiri* safely in public have recourse to certain proverbs and popular idioms that are socially acceptable. If, for instance, you wish to imply that someone is wasting time, you could classify this person's efforts as *Shiri ni megusuri*—"Putting eye-drops in his or her bottom." To imply that you or someone else has to leave posthaste, you could use *Shiri ni ho kakeru*—"Tying a sail to one's bottom." If people laugh at weaknesses that they themselves might be guilty of, you could blandly say, *Saru no shiri warai*—"One monkey laughing at another monkey's ass." To comment upon a culprit whose guilt will sooner or later surface you could quote the ostrich proverb: *Atama kakushite shiri kakusazu*—"He may hide his head, but his ass will show."

Crasser words that have gained popularity on the streets, like *ketsumedo* or *shippeta*, started off as regional dialect words before they attracted the attention of the slang crowd nationwide. *Ketsumedo* is a combination of *ketsu* and the Kansai dialect word *medo*, which literally means "aim," or "object." *Shippeta* came originally from the Oyama dialect, and specifically means "buttocks" or "buns."

> *Ichinichijū suwatte'ru kara, ketsumedo ga taresagatchimatta.*
> My ass has dropped 'cause I sit all day.
> *Ore wa shippeta o pan pan tatakareru no ga suki da!*
> I love getting my ass spanked!

Two interesting words for anus from Tokyo's red-light district are *gobō no kirikuchi*, "a cut burdock," and *kikuza*, "crysanthemum"; both expressions were originally inspired by a similarity in shape between these plants and an anus.

> *Ano sutorippā ga kagandara gobō no kirikuchi ga mieta!*
> When that stripper bent over I could see her asshole!
> *Hei beibi! Omae no kikuza namete mo ii ka?*
> Hey babe! Can I lick your ass?

KINTAMA. Balls.

In Japan a testicle is officially known as *kōgan*. The most popular word however, favored by old and young nationwide, is *kintama*, "golden balls."

Kintama is one of the few ancient Japanese slang words that have thrived throughout the centuries. Although today it is written with the characters *kin*, "gold," and *tama*, "ball," this word began its venerable career as a fusion of the characters *ki*, meaning "life," and *tama*, meaning "soul."

> *Shinjirarenē! Kanojo ore no kintama sawatte'ta! Nante onna da!*
> Man, I couldn't believe it! She grabbed my balls! What a woman!
> *Gee! Ano otoko hitomae de jibun no kintama kakimushitte'ru no mita ka yo?*
> Yuck! Did you see that man scratch his balls in front of everyone?

Another popular expression for testicles is *tama*, literally "balls." (Be careful, however; in some dialects it means "penis.")

> *Aa! Tama ga kayui nā!*
> Man! My balls itch!
> *Mizugi no waki kara tama ga miechatta!*
> I saw his balls hanging out from under his trunks!

If you need to discuss testicles in mixed company or in refined surroundings, the word to choose would be *kyūsho*. It is made up of the characters *kyū*, meaning "critical" or "crucial," and *sho*, meaning "place." As this particular expression accentuates the susceptibility of a testicle, it is favored by sports announcers and the like on those occasions when a ball inadvertently incapacitates a player during baseball, golf, or other dangerous sports.

> *Kore wa bōru ga kyūsho ni atatta yō desu ne! Itai desu ne!*
> Ooh! That ball hit him in a vulnerable spot! That must hurt!
> *Atashi kuruma no doa aketara, kare no chōdo kyūsho ni atatchatte sā! Kare'ttara shinisō datta yo!*
> When I opened the car door I hit him right in the balls! He looked like he was gonna die!

A street-wise proverb:

Teki no kyūsho wa waga kyūsho.
My enemy's "soft spot" is my "soft spot."

What you would be saying if you quoted this proverb (which by the way is of Chinese origin) is that you are well prepared for a confrontation with your opponent, as you know that his weak points are the same as yours.

Two cruder street-favorites for testicle are *oinari-san* and *oinaribukuro.*

Oinari-san is a type of sushi that originated in Osaka and looks remarkably like balls. *Oinaribukuro* is a variation of this idea, *bukuro*, "sack," referring to the roundish sack of deep-fried tofu (*abura age*) in which the vinegared sushi rice is stuffed.

Furo ga sugē atsusugite, ore nanka oinari-san yakedo suru ka to omotta!
The bath was so hot I thought I was gonna burn my balls!
Atashi, sā, kare no kemukujara no oinaribukuro ga momo ni ataru no ga suki na no.
I love it when his hairy balls rub against my thigh.

KIZA. Flashy.

Chintzy clothing, gaudy objects, or showy behavior in public are not encouraged in Japan. People in all walks of life find it safer to blend in, a practice recently titled *uii-izumu*, "we-ism," and not to stand out with the more venturous *mii-izumu*, "me-ism."

As one of Japan's most famous proverbs warns, *Deru kugi utareru*, "The nail that sticks out will be hammered down." If someone does stick out, he or she can be effectively hammered into place with a quick *kiza*, a word deriving from the characters *ki*, "spirit," and *za*, "affect" (literally "behavior that disturbs the spirit"). *Kiza* developed from *kizaru*, "spirit-disturbing," and has been a popular expression since the early Edo period (1600–1867).

> *Kono fuku de ii ka na? Chotto kiza ka na?*
> Are these clothes OK or are they too loud?
> *Nani kono kiza na kuruma! Kimochi waruku natchau!*
> What a tacky car! It's sickening!

As *kiza* is the noun and *kiza na* the adjectival form, the logical step in the direction of a verb was to add the verb-ending *"ru,"* giving us *kizaru, kiza's* most recent offspring.

> *Atashi kizaru yatsu nante issho ni dekakenai wa!*
> I'm not gonna go out with such a goofball!
> *Kono disuko de wa sonna ni kizaru no, yoshita hō ga ii wa yo!*
> You'd better stop acting up like this in this club!

Japanese street culture takes as dim a view of brash comportment as the Japanese professional classes do. Fashionable street-slang variants of *kiza* and *kizaru* are their inversions *zaki* and *zakiru.**

> *Kono doresu zaki dakedo, yo-ke-i-na-o-se-wa!*
> So what if this dress's tacky! Mind your own damn business!
> *Ano shin'iri-me yake ni zakitte yagaru! Kyōiku shite yaru ze!*
> That new guy's kinda acting up! We'll teach him a lesson or two!

In the same group of words is the popular *kebakebashii.* It is not usually written in characters, but when it is, each of the two *keba* characters is made up of a cluster of three little *ke* (hair) ideograms (giving a grand total of six "hair" characters in one word—a definite record). The resulting nuance is that the flashiness and gaudiness implicit in *kebakebashii* is likened to abundant jets of sprouting hair.

---

* *Zakiru,* by the way, also means "to have sex with" in red-light circles.

Dare ano kebakebashii gaijin no suke?
Who's that cheap foreign bimbo?
Sonna kebakebashii meiku ja soto ni dekakeraremasen!
You're not going out with such slutty make-up!

When confronted with something or someone particularly distasteful, some Japanese might find *kebakebashii* too weak and opt for the stronger *kebai* (written with the same hairy character).

Dōshita no, sono kingusari! Kebai dake jan!
What's with this gold chain? It's so tacky!
Kebai yo nē, ano chūnen jiji! Hiyake ni murasaki no nekutai shite'n no!
What a tacky old fart! With that suntan and that purple tie!

Another handy expression for censuring chintziness, also related to *kebakebashii*, is *okeba*, an expression that has become very popular in the early '90s. It is as snippy as *kebai* (its parent word), but carries a subtle dose of superciliousness with its honorific prefix *o*.

Kono sutokkingu okeba da to omou kedo, iin da!
This pantyhose's just too crass, but who cares?
Atashi anna kuso-otoko to nido to dekakenai wa! Atashi no doresu okeba da'tte itta!
I'm not going out with that asshole again! He said my dress was cheap!

The newest anti-chintz words to hit the scene zero in on cheap fashion jewelry, loud makeup, and outfits that are supposed to be the latest, but serve only to underline their wearer's gaucheness. To criticize an overabundance of fake jewelry the words to choose would be *kebajara*, "flashy glitz," or *hadejara*, "flamboyant glitz"—both words based on the onomatopoeic *jarajara*, "jingle jangle."

Kawaisō na kebajara onna! Sensu zero!
I feel sorry for that trashy-looking number! She's got zero taste!
Mite ano hadejara obatarian renchū! Sorotte minisukāto haichatte!
Look at those glitzy old bags! They're wearing miniskirts!

As a variation on the glitzy *jara* theme we have *jimijara* and *akuse jarajara.*

Jimijara literally means "plain glitz," and is reserved for plain or even ugly women who deck themselves out with heaps of glitter in the hope, as the term suggests, that some of it will rub off. *Akuse jarajara,* "accessories glitter glitter," describes the bejeweled condition itself.

Mite yo! Nante jimijara na yatsu! Koko wa saibansho yo! Kurabu ja nai!
Look what she's wearing! What a bimbo! This is a court-room, not some bar!
Kanojo wa akuse jarajara shigoto ni kita yo!
She came to work decked out like some tramp!

KURO. Opium.

The most popular word for opium on the Japanese streets is *kuro,* literally "black," a name inspired by the black, tarry texture of the drug. Opium is not considered a major drug threat in Japan (amphetamines and paint thinners top the most-wanted list), but there are cliques of opium fans all over the country who are supplied with tons of the stuff by the Yakuza gangs' import and distribution networks.

Ore kono kuro mita dake de hai ni natchimau yo!
Man, I get high just by looking at that shit!
Ittai ore-tachi kono kuro utte, ikura kasegeru to omou?
How much do you think we'll make from selling this black?

The actual word for opium in Japanese is *ahen*. It is made up of the characters *a*, for "pleasure" or "delectation," and *hen*, meaning "a piece of" or "a morsel": a morsel of happiness. Throughout Japan's history this "morsel" has cost many citizens their heads.

Opium was the first forbidden drug in Japan. It first appeared during the Muromachi period, in the fourteenth century, and was used for medicinal purposes. By the Edo period (1600–1868), recreational use of opium had become "the thing," to the extent that the authorities clamped down with the death penalty. Even today, laws in Japan are strict compared to the West. The Opium Control Act of 1948 that is in effect today—the *Ahen Torishimari Hō*—carries an average sentence of seven years just for possession.

> *Kono ahen dō surun da yo? Sū no ka?*
> What you gonna do with that opium? You gonna smoke it?
> *Wakaru darō? Kono iro to nioi! Kono ahen wa besuto da ze!*
> You can tell, man! The color, the smell—this opium's top grade!

Other casual references to opium are *nama*, meaning "raw," and *yāpin*, the Japanese pronunciation of the Chinese word for opium, *yapian*.

> *Kono nama, marifana to mikusu shite miro yo. Sugoi ze!*
> Try mixing that opium with marijuana. It's great, man!
> *Kono yāpin wa Hon Kon san da.*
> This opium's from Hong Kong.

Another popular word for opium is *tsugaru*. *Tsugaru* refers to the domestic raw opium, brown like coffee grounds, that is grown illicitly on the plains of Tsugaru, a fertile agricultural region of northern Japan.

> *Nani? Kore ga tsugaru da'tte? Iro ga hen ja nai ka?*
> What? This stuff's Tsugaru opium? Ain't the color weird?

Tsugaru ichikiro katchimaō ze! Sore de shōbai dekiru yo!
Let's get a whole kilo of this Tsugaru stuff! We can make a bundle!

Opium eaters are officially known as *ahen jōyōsha*, a formal concoction that is not particularly popular with the Japanese street crowd (try pronouncing it after a hit). Favorite street words for "opium eater" are *ahenchū, kurochū*, or *namachū* (*chū* is short for *chūdoku*, "addiction").

Atarimae da yo! Aitsu wa ahenchū sā! Me o mireba, sugu wakaru!
Of course he's an opium addict! Look at his eyes and you can tell!
Ore-tachi kono hen no kurochū ni kore ureru ze.
Let's unload this stuff on the opium freaks around here.
Anta ano namachū wa sugokatta yo! Buru buru furuete'n da mon!
Man, you should have seen that opium freak! He was like shaking all over!

Safe houses and clubs that act as "opium dens" are officially known as *ahen kyūinjo*, or more popularly as *ahen kutsu*, "opium den," or *kuro kutsu*, "black den."

Shitte'ru ka, ano Roppongi no kurabu? Ima wa mō ahen kutsu ni natta.
You know that club in Roppongi? It's turned into an opium den.
Nimotsu matomete koko dero yo! Koko wa kuro kutsu ja nēn da!
Pack your bags and get outa here! This isn't an opium den!

M

MANZURI. Female masturbation.

An interesting fact worth noting is that although American slang can boast of an overwhelming assemblage of words for male masturbation, the only current American slang words that can apply to women are "to play with oneself," "frig," and "diddle" (*Random House Thesaurus of Slang*, 1988). In the case of masturbation, Japanese slang is much more gender-equal—male and female masturbation are each represented by a rich bouquet of slang words.

Manzuri, literally "ten thousand rubs," is the most common of this group, and derives from the colloquial Japanese word for male masturbation, *senzuri*, "thousand-rubs." *Manzuri suru* or *manzuri yaru* are the customary verb forms.

> *Nē! Honto ni manzuri shitara hada ga kirei ni naru no? Ichi nichi ni nankai shinakya dame?*
> Is it true that if you play with yourself it's good for your skin? How often a day are you supposed to do it?
> *Aa! Atashi manzuri ni wa aki aki da wa! Hommono no chimpoko hoshii yo!*
> I've had enough of playing with myself! I want some real dick!

Two other variations on *manzuri* are the closely related *omankosuri* (cunt rub, also pronounced by some *omakosuri)* and its fashionable Osaka variation, *omekosuri*.

103

Ano bideo sugē ze! Omankosuri yatte'n no marumie nan da mon!

That tape's ace! This chick's giving it to herself and you can see everything!

Atashi neru mae ni maiban kanarazu omekosuri yaru!

I always bang my box a bit before I go to sleep at night!

In the same *omanko/omeko* group (these two words are the most popular slang words for vagina in Japan) are the expressions *temanko* and *temeko*, both meaning "hand-cunt."

Omē! Kanojo mechakucha temanko shita ze!

Yo man! She was really giving it to herself!

Anta-ra futari sorotte temeko shita'tsū no? Honto ka yo?

Did you girls really finger-fuck each other? Are you serious?

Two other noteworthy words for "diddling" are *bobowaru* and *nigiribobo*. The *bobo* in both words refers to the vagina, *bobo* being a popular Kyushu island dialect-slang word that has become a favorite throughout Japan. *Bobowaru* literally means "splitting the vagina"; *nigiribobo*, "grab-vagina," besides its primary allusion to "diddling," can also mean forcing one's clenched hand through the clasped thighs to reach the woman's reproductive organ.

Onna ga bobowaru no mita koto aru ka? Dō yarun darō?

Have you ever seen a woman play with herself? I wonder how they do it?

Kanojo wa ireru mae kanarazu ore ni nigiribobo saseru.

She always lets me fondle her snatch a bit before I put it in.

Two expressions favored in sex-business circles are *yubi ningyō*, "finger doll," and *yubizeme*, "finger attack." (*Ningyō*, "doll," is a euphemism for dildo.) *Yubizeme* has a broad range of meaning, especially in the jargons of Soapland massage parlors. If, for instance, the customer pays extra, the *sōpu jo*, "soap girl," will do what is also termed *yubizeme*, "finger attack," on his anus, which involves in-depth manipulation and finger penetration. By association, *yubizeme* can also be used of a customer "finger attacking" the soap girl.

> *Chotto yubi ningyō suru no wa ii yo.*
> A bit of fingering doesn't do any harm.
> *Atashi yubizeme de shika ikanain no! Boifurendo tsukaenē yo!*
> I usually just play with myself! My boyfriend's useless!

Two "frig" words that originated in the rougher areas of Tokyo are the traditional *ateire*, "blocking and entering," and the foreign-inspired *suichi o ireru*, "flicking the switch," which could be translated into American slang as "fingering a clit."

> *Atashi monogokoro tsuite kara zutto ateire shite'n no yo.*
> I've been finger-fucking myself ever since I can remember.
> *Ano sutorippā wa ore no me no mammae de suitchi o irete yagatta.*
> That stripper was fingering her clit right in front of my face.

Slang speakers are always interested in new expressions to add to their repertoire. In the case of female masturbation, some of the strongest new words have been imported from the popular Osaka dialect. Two of the important X-rated Osaka words used throughout Japan are *irou* and *irau*.

> *Shinjirareru? Jibun no asoko irau no ga suki'tte!*
> Would you believe this? She said she likes playing with her thing!
> *Jussai no koro tomodachi ga dō yatte irou no ka misete kuretan no yo.*
> When I was ten a friend showed me how to play with it.

Finally, there are a group of words that are somewhat more graphic in the sense that they focus on the hand action during masturbation and comment on its intensity.

The first rung on the ladder of intensity is *ijiru*, "to finger."

> *Mainichi ijitte'ru?*
> Do you play with yourself every day?

The next step up the ladder is *ijirimawasu*, "to finger all around."

> *Atashi odoroichatta! Ken no ijirimawashikata umain da mon!*
> *Futsū no otoko wa shiranai no ni sa!*
> I was surprised Ken was so good at playing with my twat!
> Guys usually have no idea!

A word closely related to *ijirimawasu*, but even stronger, is *ijirimakuru*, "fingering around and around."

> *Atashi itsu demo doko demo asoko o ijirimakutchau! Gaman*
> *dekinai no yo!*
> I've always got this urge to play with myself! I can't help it!

The strongest word in this progression, and the strongest "diddle" word in the Japanese language, is the explosive *ijiri-makuri-mawasu*, a word of violent intensity that English, for all its resourcefulness, could never match. Loosely translated it would read: "fingering in, out, and all around like there's no tomorrow."

MARIFANA. Marijuana.

The two most common pronunciations of marijuana in Japanese are *marifana* or *marippana*. Cannabis has been native to Japan for centuries, growing in abundance. It never crossed anyone's mind to smoke it, but it did play an important role in the daily life of the indigenous Ainus, who used it to make the cloth of their colorful costumes.

American soldiers arriving after World War II were staggered by how bountiful the crop was. There was quite a lot of high-spirited fun, which came to an abrupt end in 1948, when the commanders of the occupation force caught on, and the

Taima Torishimari Hō, the Hemp Control Act, was enforced. In Japan, marijuana abuse never reached the heights of amphetamine abuse. Even today it does not feature among the predominant drugs. Most of the cannabis in Japan is brought in from Hawaii in small quantities and is used by the younger generation as a trendy American drug.

"Doing" marijuana can be translated into Japanese as *marifana osū* or *marifana o yaru*.

> *Nē, marippana suttara chūdoku natchau ka na?*
> Do you become an addict if you smoke marijuana?
> *Kare'tte heya de marifana yatte'n da yo.*
> He's up in his room smoking pot.

The official word for marijuana is *taima*, "hemp." Past generations generally avoided the word, believing that it sounded too official to be "cool," but its repeated use in the media in the late 1980s has helped rekindle its popularity among the younger generation.

> *Kono taima yatte minai? Sugē hai ni naru yo!*
> Wanna try this marijuana? You'll get real high!
> *Suzuko ima taima sabaite'ru ze! Nyū Yōku ni kone ga aru rashii.*
> Suzuko's selling marijuana! It seems she's got a connection in New York.

Slangier synonyms for *taima* and *marifana* are *kusa*, "grass," and *happa*, "leaves." These words parallel the American slang expressions "grass" and "weed," and are just as popular in Japan.

> *Oi, omē! Kono kusa no nioi kaide miro yo! Kore wa zettai saikōkyūhin da ze!*
> Yo, man! Take a whiff of this grass! Top grade stuff!
> *Ano happa sugē tsuyokute, ore kura kura shita yo! Honto da ze!*
> That weed was *so* strong I was like hallucinating! I'm serious!

The newest word for marijuana on the streets, *choko*, came from the high-school crowd.

> *Ii choko ja nai? Dok' kara mitsuketa no?*
> Great marijuana. Where did you find it?
> *Choko yatta ato 'tte, mō hara ga hete hara ga hete shō ga nē yo nā.*
> After we smoked that weed we got the strongest munchies.

An important marijuana-related verb is *maku*, "to roll," as in "rolling a joint."

> *Happa makeru dake nokotte'ru ka na?*
> Do we have enough grass to roll a joint?
> *Happa no makikata shitte'ru?*
> You know how to roll a joint?

Another popular way of referring to marijuana is by its country of origin, by adding the word *san*, or "product of," to the country's name. Three typical types of "grass" are *Hawai san*, "Hawaiian," *Tai san*, "Thai," and *Indo san*, "Indian."

> *Indo san yatta koto aru? Sugē ii yo!*
> Ever done Indian grass? It's ace!
> *Kinō Tai san yattara sugē buttonjimatta!*
> We did some Thai yesterday and got seriously fucked up, man!
> *Hawai san no hō ga ore wa suki da nā.*
> Me, my favorite's the Hawaiian stuff.

The Japanese equivalent to the American "pothead" or "user" is *happachū*, "leaf addict," *kusachū*, "grass addict," or *happaboke*, "grass doter." *Boke* is a suffix usually reserved for victims of the harder drugs, especially amphetamines. Used in reference to someone who indulges in lighter stuff, it has a comical nuance of overstatement.

Omē ichinichijū kore suttara happachū ni naru no wa atari-mae da!
Of course you're gonna turn into a pothead if you smoke this all day!
Aitsu sonna ni kusachū de itain dattara, hott'okeba! Ore-tachi ni kankei nē kara!
If he wants to be a total pothead let him! It's not our problem!
Aitsu happaboke da yo na.
This guy's a regular grass fiend.

MUNE. Breast.

Traditionally, *mune* refers to an unspecified region of the human torso from approximately the stomach area to the larynx. It is involved in many colloquial phrases, such as *mune ga doki doki suru*, "my heart throbs," *mune ga warui* (the stomach is bad), "to be sickened by something," or *mune ga sawagu* (the chest clamors), "to be excited." Besides these everyday idioms, to the exasperation of traditional language purists, *mune* is increasingly being used by the modern generation to mean "tits."

Kanojo no mune wa saikō da ze!
Her tits are first class!
Ore saisho ni me ni tsuku no ga mune nan da yo na.
The first thing I look at are a woman's breasts.

A non-dictionary word that ranks with the most important slang words for breasts is *oppai*.

Anta atashi no oppai momitai? Ii wa yo!
Wanna feel my breasts? Go ahead!
Kanojo kagandara oppai marumie da yo!
When she bends over you can see her breasts!

Ingo (hidden language), which is the Japanese name for criminal street slang, has a habit of inverting words to render them incomprehensible to outsiders. *Oppai*, which is written in the Japanese hiragana syllabary as *o-tsu-pai* was inverted to create *paiotsu*.

> *Ano onna no paiotsu beron beron ni tarete'ru yo!*
> That woman's bazookas are dangling all the way down!
> *Betsu no onna yonde koi! Koitsu no paiotsu ja monotarinē!*
> Get me another girl! This one's tits aren't big enough!

Two words that were created from *oppai* to specify very small breasts are the veteran street word *pechapai*, "flat breast," and the newer high-school Anglo-Japanese hybrid *rēzunpai*, "raisin pie." The concept behind "raisin pie" is a breast so small that it could be characterized as a raisin. The word *rēzunpai* also qualifies as a deft pun on the popular raisin-pie cake.

> *Earobikusu shisugiru kara kanojo pechappai ni kimatte'ru yo.*
> I'm not surprised she's got no boobs, what with all the aerobics she's doing.
> *Dō yū imi da yo, rēzunpai nante! Anta no, nanka, koyubi no saki gurai ja nai yo!*
> How dare you call me flat when my pinky's bigger than your dick!

One of the more hazardous *oppai* concoctions is the red-light-district expression *paizuri*, literally "breast-urbation." This service is expensive, but it is available in every self-respecting Soapland massage parlor. The *paizuri* service involves the *sōpu jo* (soap girl) clasping the client's sexual organ between her breasts and bringing him to a climax with adroit jolts.

A traditional synonym for *paizuri* still very popular in today's sex clubs in Japan is the poetic *tanima no shirayuri*, "white lily in the valley," the white lily being the sperm that would end up between the breasts, which are metaphorically seen as "the valley." A more modern rendering of this vintage term is its loose rendition into English as *on za hiru*, or "on the hill."

N

NAMA. Condomless.

In Japan, condoms are the most important form of contraception. Using condoms was the common practice long before the West launched its safe-sex campaigns of the 1980s. As a result, sex *au naturel* is regarded as a special delicacy.

Nama, "raw," originated in the *akasen*, the "red-line" district, where the munificent client could request exclusive "raw" service, involving sex or fellatio without a condom.

> *Atashi nama dewa shinai! Datte ninshin shitaku nai mon!*
> I'm not gonna do it without a condom! I don't wanna get pregnant!
> *Nama de yarō ze! Ore chan to iku mae ni nuku kara yo!*
> Let's do it without a condom! I promise to pull out just before I come!

Also related to *nama* (raw) is the more potent *junnama*, "pure raw," a word coined by the condomless-sex enthusiasts of the Soapland massage parlors and the sex clubs.

> *Ore kane ōme ni haratta kara junnama yareta.*
> I paid a lot, so I got to do it without a condom.
> *Kondōmu torina! Junnama de yarō!*
> Take the rubber off! We'll do it without!

The other favorite slang expression for no-condom sex, *zatōichi*, originated in a more unlikely quarter, a popular Japanese children's television series. Its story takes place in the good old Samurai days, with Zatoichi, the kind but bellicose leading man, ever ready to rescue a damsel in distress.

What made Mr. Zatōichi an exemplary candidate for the allusion to condomless sex was the fact that his trademark was the unsheathed sword—ever ready for action.

> *Atashi baka dakara ninshin shichatta yo! Aitsu ni zatōichi sasechatta kara!*
> Idiot that I am, I got pregnant! I let him do it without a rubber!
> *Zatōichi shitai'tte? Ryōkin wa nibai yo!*
> You wanna do it without? It'll cost you double!

The most indelicate synonym for *nama* (raw) is *sumara*, "bare penis."

> *Atashi nan da to omotte'n da! Otokui-san dake sumara sasete yarun dakara!*
> What do you think I am! It's only special customers I let do it without a rubber!
> *Ore kyō dōshite mo sumara yaritē!*
> Man, I really wanna do it without the party hat today!

When it comes to fellatio in the red-light district, the norm would be *fera kabuse*, "fellatio-covered," or *surippu*, "slip," a punny contraction of *sukin-rippu sābisu*, "skin (condom)-lip service."

During these trying times, "uncovered" is classified as a very expensive *supesharu sābisu* (special service). Two of the favorite designations for this type of fellatio are *nama ensō*, "live performance," and *namajaku*. *Namajaku* is a contraction of the longer *nama shakuhachi*, and literally means "raw *shakuhachi* flute." The *shakuhachi* is a vertical flute that is blown like a clarinet, and for centuries it has been a favorite red-light metaphor for fellatio.

> *Anta mō nama ensō yametara? Saikin ironna byōki aru jan.*
> Shouldn't you stop sucking guys off? There's all kindsa diseases out there.
> *Warui kedo, atashi namajaku yaranai! Hai kondōmu!*
> Sorry, I only suck dick if you wear a rubber! Here's one!

NEKURA. Depressed or negative.

While a young American is "down," "in a blue funk," or has assumed a "prune face," a young Japanese with similar symptoms is diagnosed by his fashionable friends as *nekura*. This new, modish word originated from the phrase *ne ga kurai*, "the root is dark," and is closely related to its equally "in" antonym *neaka*, "bright-rooted," reserved for peppy and positive individuals. Actually, in these cases "root" refers to a person's character, personality, or nature.

> *Kanojo'tte itsumo nekura na no? Soretomo ima dake?*
> Has she always been so negative, or is it new?
> *Sonna ni nekura ni natte 'nai de! Odorō ze! Tanjōbi jan!*
> Don't be so depressing! C'mon let's dance! It's your birthday!

Nekura gave rise to the school-slang abbreviation *nekku*, also meaning "blue," or "in the dumps."

> *Hott'okeba! Ano ko kyō nekku!*
> Lay off it, man! The poor kid's in the dumps!
> *Atashi anta sonna ni nekku ni naru toki daikirai!*
> I hate it when you get so bummed!

A high-school favorite that has oozed out into club-scene talk is *kuradishonaru*, which together with its peers *nekura* and *nekku* also belongs to the *kurai* ("dark" or "gloomy") clan. Like many of the most "in" Japanese slang words today, it is an Anglo-Japanese alloy, a fusion of *kurai* and *toradishonaru*, "traditional."

The poor individual for whom *kuradishonaru* is reserved is regarded as gloomy and depressed precisely because he or she is "traditional," which in modern Japan is tantamount to being "just too uncool for words."

> *Kuradishonaru gyaru nante dēto shitaku nai.*
> I don't wanna go on a date with such a nerdy girl.

Kanojo debu da shi, busu da shi, kuradishonaru da shi, moderu naritai shi! Saiaku!
She's fat, she's ugly, she's a nerd, and she wants to be a model! P-l-l-l-ease!

A depressed person who lounges about emitting plaintive groans and acts like a wet blanket at congenial get-togethers could be denounced in fashionable if slangy Japanese with the verb *būtareru*. The etymology of this novel expression is *bū*, as in *bū bū yū*, "to complain" or "to grumble," and *tareru*, "to drop" or "to let go."

Sonna ni būtareru na yo!
Stop whining!
Ano ko ni tomodachi ga inai no mo atarimae da yo na! Itsumo būtareru kara sa!
I'm not surprised that girl has no friends! She's always pissing and moaning!

Another unfortunate state to be in is what is known as *busukureru*. The depressed, down-and-out individual is so devastated about something or other that his face clenches up in a sour grimace—the derivation of *busukureru* is *busu*, "ugly," and *kureru*, "to be overcome with" or "to abandon oneself to."

Busukureru no yamero yo! Chan to meiku shite, issho ni dekakeyō ze!
Why don't you just get over it! Put some makeup on and let's hit the scene!
Uchi no kurasu no onna-domo minna busukurete bakkari ite! Zenzen tsumannē!
Those girls in our class are such downers! They're a total drag!

Another *wakamono* (young generation) word reserved for the saturnine or the morose is *yande'ru*, originating from *yamu*, "to be taken ill."

Yande'ru yatsu!
What a grim guy!

114

Kono ongaku honto yande'ru yo!
This music's just too down!

A stronger word reserved for a truly dismal state of affairs is *do-tsubo,* "large pot." It is a hardy slang word that is used as readily by a Yakuza boss when things go wrong as by a thirteen-year-old schoolgirl miffed about having failed her exams. A typical idiomatic usage would be *do-tsubo ni hamaru,* "to fall into a large pot."

> *Ore moshi kotoshi daigaku ni hairenakattara, jinsei do-tsubo da yo na!*
> If I don't get into college this year, my life'll be the pits!
> *Kanojo himo to ōgenka shichatte! Mō do-tsubo!*
> She had a big row with her pimp! She's in for it!

NINSHIN. Pregnancy.

Ninshin suru, "to become pregnant," and *ninshin shite iru,* "to be pregnant," are the standard expressions for pregnancy appropriate at any social level, from medical circles and joyfully expectant mothers to the street crowd and not-so-joyfully expectant mothers. Both of the characters that make up the word *ninshin* contain the ideogram for woman: *nin,* a combination of "woman" and "duty," and *shin,* "woman" and "time"; the idea is that pregnancy is the time a woman fulfills her duty.

> *Anta nanka okashii yo! Ninshin shitan ja nai no?*
> You're acting strange! You're not pregnant, are you?

The other standard dictionary term for pregnancy is *haramu,* "to become pregnant," or "to concieve." The character for *haramu* is made up of the elements "with" and "child," and is the older native Japanese term. While *ninshin* is flexible in meaning, *haramu* has adverse nuances in contemporary speech. Depending on the tone of voice, *Aa! Ninshin shichatta!* could mean "Oh, I'm pregnant! (Let's celebrate!)" or "Oh, I'm pregnant! (Darn!)." *Aa! Kodomo haranjatta!*, however, "I've conceived a child," has a definite ring of despair to it.

> *Nē! Haranjatta koto aru?*
> Have you ever gotten pregnant?
> *Kodomo harande'ru to dō yū fū ni naru no?*
> What if I get pregnant?

If a modern Japanese high school girl or college student gets pregnant, and she breaks down and confesses to her girlfriends, she would most probably opt for the fashionable euphemism *tomaru*, "to stop," as in "my period stopped."

> *Chikusho! Mata tomatchatta!*
> Fuck! I'm expecting again!
> *Aitsu tiinējā no kuse ni tomaru nante!*
> She's just a damn teenager and she's pregnant!

Another new word for pregnancy in Japanese high-school yards is *sairen*, "siren." As the word suggests, from the pregnant person's point of view "the delicate condition" is synonymous with disaster or catastrophe.

> *Atashi kensa shinakya! Tabun sairen da wa!*
> I've gotta take the test! I think I'm preg!
> *Nē, ii byōin shiranai? Kanojo sairen nan da yo nē.*
> You know a good clinic? She's expecting.

A foreign-inspired neologism popular with younger slang speakers is the Anglo-Japanese *inharabebii*. To anatomize this cryptic word we can break it down into its three elements: *in*, the English "in," *hara*, Japanese for "belly," and *bebii*, English for "baby": the result *in-hara-bebii*, "in-belly-baby."

> *Kanojo esu da to omotte'tara, inharabebii da'tte yo!*
> I thought she was a dyke—and she's expecting!
> *Kanojo no inharabebii dare no sei darō?*
> Who knocked her up?

116

A pseudo-English expression that was launched by the bright young Tokyo set is *dii rain*, as in *D* line (if you inspect the stomach of an expecting mother you will notice, as the Tokyo set did, that its outline brings to mind a capital *D*).

> *Kanojo dii rain na no ka na, soretomo futotta no ka na?*
> Is she pregnant, or just fat?
> *Atashi sekkusu raifu wa dii rain ni natte mo zenzen kawannai!*
> Even though I'm preg my sex life's still going strong!

An important imported American slang term is *nokku*, "knock," a doctored version of the vintage term "to knock up" (since the 1920s the most popular American slang word for pregnancy).

> *Kondo wa dare ga nokku shita no? Ken?*
> Who knocked you up this time? Ken?
> *Mata nokku sarechatta yo! Mata orosanakya!*
> I got knocked up again! I'm gonna have to get another abortion!

Another interesting English word requisitioned by the Tokyo street crowd and adapted to modern Japanese slang semantics is *panku*, short for "puncture," in this case meaning "to give birth."

> *Itsu kanojo panku suru no?*
> When's she giving birth?
> *Atashi takushii de panku shisō ni natta yo!*
> I almost had the baby in the cab!

The truly vicious street words for pregnancy are of native Japanese stock. Foreign or foreign-inspired words have the redeeming quality of a fashionable, formalistic texture; plain-spoken Japanese words don't. One of the newer words in this group is *harabote*, "stomach-heavy," a term that has a youthful but delinquent tone to it.

Atashi ki o tsukenakya! Harabote ni naritaku nai mon!
I must be careful, I don't wanna get a bun in the oven!
Harabote ni natchimatte kara ore ni nanimo yarasenai!
Since she's been pregnant she won't let me do anything!

Two older all-Japanese favorites from the *ingo* (hidden language) argot circles are the incisively vulgar *mosagamaru*, "to catch in the gut," and *garikamaru*, "to catch a child."

Anta oppai dekaku natte'n ja nai? Mosagamatte'n ja nē no?
Your tits have gotten bigger, right? Are you knocked up or something?
Ano onna garikamaru no wa chotto babāsugirun ja nai?
Isn't she's a bit over the hill to be pregnant?

In the same group with the coarsest words for pregnancy we find the related *yaripon* and *rāpon*. Of the two, *yaripon*, an amalgam of *yaru*, "to have sex," and *pon pon*, "tummy," is the fiercer. *Rāpon* has a humorously redeeming quality: *ra* being short for *rāji*, the Japanese pronunciation of the English "large," with *pon pon* added to it.

Nande yaripon natta no?
How did you get bumped?
Atashi o rāpon ni shiyagatte! Ano buta yarō koroshite yaru!
He fuckin' knocked me up! I'm gonna kill the asshole!

At the top of the pile of vulgar street words for pregnancy is *kotsubo*, a superlatively uncouth reference to the womb, literally "child pot."

Kotsubo ga dekai no ni, ano onna mada ironna otoko to nete'ru!
Even though she's knocked up she's still sleeping around!
Kotsubo ni nanka iru kara, atashi zutto guai warui no yo ne!
Since I've been knocked up I've been feeling sick as a dog!

NUSUMU. To steal.

Nusumu is the standard word for stealing. It can be used in general for most types of theft. The character for *nusu* is written with the two ideograms "next" and "plate," suggesting that the primary idea when the character was originally composed in China was swiping food from someone else's plate.

> *Anta kore doko kara nusunda no?*
> Where did you steal that from?
> *Atashi no sukāto nusunda deshō? Kaeshina yo!*
> You stole my skirt, right? Give it back!

The other main phrase for stealing is *dorobō suru. Dorobō* can mean both "thief" and "theft." It originated as a contraction of the somewhat blasphemous *toru bōzu*, "filching priest." Today *dorobō* is written in two ways: *doro*, "mud" and *bō*, "priest," and more recently and less sacrilegiously: *doro*, "mud" and *bō*, "stick."

> *Aitsu wa dōtokushin no kakera mo nē! Mitamono nandemo dorobō yagaru!*
> That guy's got no morals! He'll steal anything that's in front of him!
> *Atashi tatta no nifun kuruma hanareta dake na no ni, kuruma dorobō sarechatta yo!*
> I just left the car there for two minutes and it was stolen!

When someone "pilfers," "swipes," or "rips off" smaller objects, the *mot juste* is *kapparau*. It originally evolved from the two words *kaku*, "to scratch," and *harau*, "to brush together": the image of the character suggesting a feverish scraping together of goods, followed by a dash for the open.

> *Ano yarō ore no tokei mata kapparaiyagatte! Bukkorosu!*
> That asshole swiped my watch again! I'm gonna kill him!
> *Dare ga anta no saifu kapparatta no? Shitte'ru?*
> Who filched your wallet, d'you know?

In the same crowd of common light-theft words is a term of somewhat ruder etymology, *nekobaba*, "cat shit."

When an individual is guilty of "cat shitting," the implication is that he has "pocketed" or "copped" small but important things, usually money. The inspiration for "cat shitting" as a synonym for swiping is that cats quickly cover their tracks after defecating and act as if nothing happened.

> *Shinjirarenē! Ittai ikura aitsu nekobaba shiyagattan da?*
> I don't believe this! How much did this guy swipe?
> *Ano shin'iri no onna, reji no kane zettai nekobaba shite'run dakara!*
> That new woman keeps filching money from the register!

The main word for shoplifting is *mambiki*. In modern times it is written with the characters *man*, "ten thousand," and *hiku*, "to snatch," but it originated as the rural term *ma ni hiku*, "thinning out vegetables in a field" (literally "taking from in between").

> *Saikin mambiki yarinikui yo nē! Ironna tokoro ni kamera wa tsuite'ru shi sā!*
> Shoplifting's becoming kinda hard lately! There's all kinda cameras and stuff!
> *Shinu hodo hazukashii yo! Obā-chan mambiki shite'ru toki tsukamatchatte sā!*
> I thought I was gonna die, I was so embarrassed! They caught granny shoplifting!

A slangier synonym for shoplifting, favored by the younger street crowd, is *chomboru*, inspired by the expression *chombo*, "mistake" or "lapse."

> *Ano kuchibeni anta chombotta yatsu?*
> Is that the lipstick you filched?
> *Omē yo! Kanojo chomboru no ga sugē hayēn da ze! Uaa!*
> Dude! She's ace at swiping stuff! Wow!

The young criminal set often prefers not to call a spade a spade, or in this case filching filching. This penchant is clearly visible in what are at the moment some of the "in" street euphemisms for stealing, *kau*, "to buy," *kaimono suru*, "to go shopping," and the ominous *shigoto ni iku*, "to go to work."

> *Nani, kono meiku zembu katta? ïkagen ni shiro yo!*
> What, you "bought" all that makeup? I wish you wouldn't do that!
> *Aitsu resutoran de kegawa no kōto sanchaku kaimono shita no.*
> He swiped three fur coats from that restaurant.
> *Shigoto ni itte kuru yo.*
> I'm just going on a quick job.

Another street word for shoplifting is *dekigokoro*, "sudden impulse." As the word suggests, it is an unpremeditated act: you see it, you want it, you swipe it.

> *Sūpā ni iku to dōshite mo dekigokoro shitaku natchau!*
> Whenever I go down to the supermarket I get this urge to filch things!
> *Shinjirarenai! Ano obatarian dekigokoro shichau nante!*
> I can't believe that old bitch swipes things!

The most vivid words for theft in Japanese belong to *ingo*, "the hidden language" of the underworld. These words are thieves' "shop talk" and not generally understood off the streets. An example is *warau*, "to laugh," as in: *Kore waratta?* (You laughed that?), "You stole that?"

> *Omē ga waratta kuruma kakuii jan!*
> The car you swiped's real cool!
> *Omae waratta mon' doko ni kakushite'n da yo?*
> Where d'you stash the stuff you boosted?

In the same class of *ingo* words we have *tsumu*, "to pluck," and *giru*, short for *negiru*, "to drive a bargain."

Ore tsunda mono zembu utte, chitto kane kasegō to motte'ru.
I'm gonna sell all the stuff I ripped off and make a bit of
money.
Kono kane zembu dok'kara gittan da?
Where did you swipe all this cash from?

O

OKAMA. Homosexual.

This is the most widely used derogatory word for homosexual in Japan, parallel to English expressions like "fag," or "faggot." *Okama* originated from the word *kama*, a word for "rice pot" in use since the Heian period (794–1185).

The first step in its development into the modern slang word was when dialects like Harima, Ibaragi, Toyama, and Yamaguchi added the honorific *o* prefix and decreed it to mean posterior.* From this, by somewhat unkind association, the slang word for "homosexual" crystallized.

> *Soko no okama omē no koto zutto mite'ru ze.*
> That faggot there keeps looking at you.
> *Okama datta'tte? Kekkon shite'ru to omote'tta!*
> He's a faggot? I thought he was married!

In order to soften the untoward connotation of the noun *okama*, some people opt for the politer *Okama-san*, "Mr. Faggot." Although *Okama-san* may be a modest gesture towards being civil, the modern and the open-minded prefer the more neutral *gei*, "gay."

> *Ano hito okama-san yo.*
> That gentleman is a fag.

---

* Some dialects, notably the Sanno, the Ōtawara, the Hagagun, and the Kamitogagun, regarded the *kama* rice pot, with the added *o* prefix, as more representative of the vagina, while the Shizuoka and the Kumamoto dialects use it as a general synonym for "hole." The Ashikaga dialect went its own way using *kama* to mean "dark, hidden, secret."

Kono bā wa okama-san shika inai yo. Hoka ni ikō.
This bar is full of queers! Let's go someplace else!

When something or someone behaves in a "gay" or "faggoty" manner, *okama* can be changed into an adjective using suffixes like *-ppoi*, *-rashii*, and *-kusai* to create *okama-ppoi*, "faggot-ish," *okama-rashii*, "faggot-like," and *okama-kusai*, "smelling of faggot."

Anta sonna okama-ppoku odoranakya ii no ni!
I wish you wouldn't dance like such a fruitcake!
Aitsu-ra okama-rashikunai?
Don't you think they're faggoty?
Nande minna ore no koto okama-kusai'tte iun darō?
Why does everyone think I'm a faggot?

A more modern *okama* adjective is the witty high-school invention *okama-chikku*, literally "faggot-ic," the *-chikku* ending having been borrowed from the word *romanchikku*, or "romantic."

Nē! Omē sonna okama-chikku na no yamete kurenai?
Will you cut that faggoty shit?
Nē! Ano ko no onii-san okama-chikku yo nē! Kitto sō da yo!
You know, that girl's brother's kinda faggoty! He must be one!

A very popular deprecatory word implying that the homosexual in question is passive and/or effeminate is *onē*, "sister," often used in gay circles in its vocative form *Onē-san!* as a cute and girlish form of address.

Nani ano debu no onē! Ittai nani mono!
Get a load of that fat queen! Who does she think she is?
Onē-san! Mite, mite! Oishisō!
Ooh, girl! Look at that one! Cute!

A homosexual slang word that is practical for establishing who is passive and who is not, especially in chance encounters, is *ukemi*, literally "receiving body."

Anta ukemi?
You like to get it?
Mayonaka sugi ni, ukemi wa minna ano bā e kuridasun da.
After midnight all the queens get together at that bar.

Another highly popular Japanese word for "queen" is *neko*, "cat." By extension *neko yaru*, "to do cat," has become popular in street slang to mean gay sex, or in a broader sense "kinky sex."

Ano neko itsumo kao no ii otoko mono ni suru! Dō yarun darō?
That fruit always gets good-looking guys! How does she do it?
Kinō no ban ore Ken to sugē neko yacchimatta!
Last night I got real down and dirty with Ken!

The opposite of *neko* is *tachiyaku*. While a *neko* is effeminate, elegant, and possibly made up and in drag, the *tachiyaku* is the masculine, "active" homosexual. *Tachiyaku* is a long-standing expression from the Japanese Kabuki theater signifying the dynamic male role—the fighter with his sword ready for action.

An interesting variation is *netachi*, a melding of *neko* and *tachiyaku*. The *netachi* is the homosexual who acts butch, but when push comes to shove prefers the passive role (much to the dismay of the *neko*).

Nē, mite! Ano tachiyaku hoshii wa! Oishisō jan!
Ooh, look! I want that hunk! He's cute!
Anna otoko yamena! Netachi yo!
Forget that guy! He's just a queen!

One of the favorite gay slang terms for the bisexual man in Japanese is the vintage *ryōtōzukai*, "using both swords." Popular with the rougher *hādokoa* ("hard-core") crowd is the more down-to-earth word *ura-omote*, "bottom-top." *Ura-omote* actually has two meanings. Besides signifying "AC/DC" it can also apply to the homosexual who takes no position about assuming the active or the passive role in a gay sex encounter.

Aitsu kanojo dekita mitai dakedo, honto wa ryōtōzukai nan da ze.
Even though I think he's got a girlfriend, he's bi.
Aaa! Yappari ura-omote! So omotta yo!
So, he's AC/DC! Yeah, I thought so!

The hermaphrodite is characterized in formal Japanese as *ryōsei*, "both sexes." In street slang the preferred term is *futanari*, "both appearances."

Ano sutorippā honto no onna mitai datta no ni, jitsu wa futanari datta ze!
That stripper looked like a real woman, but it was a he-she!
Futanari ga suki na otoko'tte ippai irun da ze! Jōdan ja nē yo!
There seem to be a lotta guys here into she-males! It's just too gross!

The sex-change operation is formally known as *sei tenkan*, "sex conversion." The less formal term is *maki maki suru*, "doing maki maki," inspired by Karuseru Maki, a notorious Japanese "sex convert." This metamorphosis is known in rougher street-slang circles as *ragiri*, "penis cutting." *Ra* is short for *mara*, a popular uncouth word for "penis," and *giri* comes from *kiru*, "to cut."

Ore omae zettai wakaranai to omou yo! Aitsu maki maki shita kara marude hommono mitai.
I don't think you can tell! Since that sex change she looks like the real thing.
Moshi anta ragiri shichattara honto ni kanjiru no kashira?
If you get it cut off I wonder if you can feel anything?

OMANKO. Vagina.

Omanko is to Japanese what "cunt" is to English. Both words are of ancient lineage and started off as legitimate words that, as some experts argue, date back to the Stone Age. In the

Western hemisphere, "cunt" enjoys an illustrious pedigree, with forerunners such as the Latin *cunnus*, Old Frisian *kunte*, Old Norse *kunta*, and, astonishingly enough, the Basque word *kuna*. *Omanko*, it is argued, has an even more distinguished background, although its exact etymology is still hotly wrangled over in Japanese scholastic circles. *O*, all sides agree, is the euphemistic honorific which is sometimes dispensed with for an earthier effect (As in *manko yarō ze!*—"Let's get us some cunt!").

After this initial point of agreement the wrangle of the linguists begins. "Where does *omanko's man* come from?" is the burning question.

One of the most outlandish among many amusing theories was advanced by the eccentric South American Japanologist F. Perez de Vega. Staunchly believing that the Inca Empire was founded by ancient Japanese warriors, he argues that the *man* of *omanko* comes from the Guarani Indians in Ecuador, *man* being their word for "spirit."

An even more outlandish theory was recently published in *Nihongo wa Doko kara Kita Ka?* (Where Did Japanese Come From?) by Kawasaki Shinji, who belongs to the renegade school of thought that Japan was colonized by the ancient Egyptians, and that consequently Japanese is a Sumerian language. *Man*, he testifies, started out as the Sumerian word *man* meaning "womb."

Notwithstanding its disputed pedigree, today *omanko* is the most popular term in Japan for the female organ.

> *Kono bideo de onna no omanko honto ni marumie da ze!*
> In this video you can see this woman's cunt head-on!
> *Kanojo no omanko wa itsumo jūshii da!*
> Her cunt's always juicy!

What *omanko* is to standard Japanese, *omeko* is to the Osaka dialect. In the unlikely event that it is written in characters, the characters *me*, woman, and, *ko*, "child," are used. The exact etymology of this word is also in dispute. One of the more interesting ideas, offered by Yamanaka Jōta in *Osaka Kotoba*

127

(Osaka Speech), suggests that the word was hatched as a slang expression at the foot of the statue of the god Omeko Daikoku in Osaka, when increasing numbers of devotees noticed that the god's right hand, clenched in a fist, showed the thumb protruding between the index and middle finger, a rather rude gesture evocative of the female organ.*

Outside the Osaka dialect, *omeko* is now fashionable when a rougher, cruder alternative to *omanko* is called for.

> *Nande atashi no omeko kayukute shōganai no ka na?*
> I wonder why my snatch is so itchy?
> *Na! Hima dattara komban omeko-gari ni ikō ze!*
> Hey, if you've got time let's go pussy hunting tonight!

Two other nationwide favorites for the female organ from the Osaka dialect are *soso* and *ososo*.

Originally, these words were exclusively used by women as a euphemism. They developed from *sore sore*, "that that," into what was at the time an even meeker *so so*. Today few users of *soso* are aware of its demure background, and they savor it for its attractive alliterative quality. But beware! Regardless of their euphemistic past, *soso* and *ososo* have the same jarring impact on the well-bred Japanese ear as *omeko* or *omanko*.

> *Jūbun nurenai toki, soso ni kuriimu tsukerun da.*
> If I don't get wet I put cream on my snatch.
> *Sekken de ososo arau no kirai. Datte kasa kasa ni natchau yo.*
> I hate washing my pussy with soap. It gets all like dried out.

Another all-Japan megahit slang word for vagina is *bobo*, which comes from the island of Kyushu. Like *soso* and *ososo*, *bobo* owes much of its success in red-light districts to its upbeat, alliterative ring.

An elaboration on *bobo* is *sarabobo*, which can have two meanings: "new *bobo*," meaning the organ of a virgin, or very

---

* According to Kawasaki Shinji, *omeko* also originated in Ancient Egypt as the Sumerian word *mi*, "vagina," before it found its way into the Osaka dialect.

young woman, or "plate *bobo*," in which case the organ in question is "platelike" (i.e., wide but not deep).

> *Aitsu neta ato demo, zettai ni bobo misete kurenai.*
> Even after we slept together she still doesn't let me see her pussy.
> *Shojo no sarabobo'tte shimari ga ii kara ii yo na!*
> The great thing about a virgin's twat is that it's nice and tight!

Another noteworthy onomatopoeic word for vagina is *bebe*, a word that originated in the Oyama, Kanuma, Ōtawara, and Yaita dialects.* *Bebe* belongs to the same group of red-light terms that, due to their charismatic ring, have risen from the comparative obscurity of the provinces to national notoriety. *Bebe* has the advantage over *bobo* and *soso* of sounding foreign, if not French.

> *Aitsu atashi no bebe ni dake kyōmi arun da yo ne! Futsū no otoko dakara ne!*
> All he's interested in is my snatch! Typical of men!
> *Ore sutorippā no me no mae ni suwatta kara yo! Bebe marumie datta!*
> Man! I sat right in front of that stripper! I could see her twat inside out!

Two other vulgar but popular words for vagina are *kanko* and *okanko*, originally from the Sanno dialect. They are favored throughout the nation because they rhyme with the standard words for vagina, *manko* and *omanko*.

> *Hajime no uchi kanojo no kanko ga kawaite'ta kara chotto itakatta.*
> At first it hurt a bit 'cause her cunt was dry.
> *Atashi okanko ni tampon ireru toki no kanji daikirai!*
> I hate the feeling of a tampon up my cunt!

---

* Its close relatives *hehe* and *pepe* did not make it on the national scene, part of the reason being that in some villages, confusingly enough, they also mean "penis" or "sexual intercourse."

129

Among the provincial words that have made it onto the city streets there are also expressions, rampant in red-light quarters, that are not as widely known as their onomatopoetic relatives. *Sane* is one of these words for vagina; it arrived on the national slang scene after enjoying widespread popularity in the Yaita and Utsunomiya dialects. Another word for the female organ is *shimo*, which was actually inspired by one of the alternative pronunciations of the character for "down" (usually read *shita*).

> *Chotto sane hippa'nno yamete yo! Itai jan!*
> Will you stop tugging at my snatch! It hurts!
> *Kono mizugi katta kedo kirenai yo! Shimo marumie!*
> I can't wear this swim suit I bought! You can see my crack!

ORUGASUMU. Orgasm.

In the 1870s, German doctors arriving in Japan as part of the Meiji-era Westernization brought with them German medical terms like *shokku*, for "shock," *asupirin*, for "asprin," and *orugasumusu*, from the German *Orgasmus*, which, by the way, is still the official Japanese dictionary word. (Aside from euphemisms such as *saikōchō*, "climax" or "peak," and *kyokudo no kōfun*, "extreme excitement," Japanese has no official native words for orgasm.)

Since its introduction into Japanese, *orugasumusu* has been treated with all the deference appropriate to a long-winded foreign medical term that was thought to sound too authoritative for colloquial speech. This changed when the media and fashionable magazines developed an interest in orgasm and started using *orugasumu*, a shortened version of the German original, or *ōgasumu*, the Japanese pronunciation of the English word. As some magazines might write:

Hajimete no sekkusu de orugasumu o erareru koto wa mazu arimasen.
During one's first sexual experience it is very rare to experience orgasm.
Naze watashi wa ōgasumu o kanjinai no deshō?
Why can I not experience orgasm?

With the gentle prompting of the popular question-and-answer sections of teen magazines and other popular periodicals that offer sexual advice and enlightenment, the two semi-official words for "orgasm," *ōgasumu* and *orugasumu*, now appear in slangier speech.

Kanojo wa ōgasumu ni tasshita toki, sugē uairudo ni natta.
When she had her orgasm she went totally wild.
Kinō yokatta ze! Kanojo to ore dōji ni orugasumu kanjita mon!
Yesterday was great! We had an orgasm at the same time!

In relaxed conversation Japanese slang speakers often prefer stronger native words. One of the more unconventional but pithy terms for orgasm used on the streets is *rariru*, "to flip out," a term usually connected with a drug high.

Atashi itsumo raritta furi shite'ru kara, kare manzoku nan da!
I always pretend to get off just to make him feel good!
Ore-tachi pettingu shite'ta dake na no ni, ore raritchatta!
Although we were just making out I really shot my wad!

A strong slang word from the red-light district, used exclusively in reference to male orgasm, is *naku*, "to cry" or "to howl." This expression is usually used by the "soap girls" of the Soapland establishments and by sex-club hostesses in discussing their clientele's orgasms.

Kyaku no asoko yasashiku ijitte yaru to, motto hayaku nakaserareru yo.
If you rub your client's dick gently, chances are he'll shoot his wad quicker.

Anta mō naichatta no? Hayasugi ja nai?
What, you got off already? That was a bit quick, wasn't it?

A special term reserved for those times when a couple reach orgasm simultaneously is *hamoru*, an idiom borrowed from the show-business world, where it is used to refer to successful musical harmonizing between a male and a female singer.

Atashi hamonnai toki wa kirai.
I hate it when we don't come together.
Sekkusu de ichiban no pointo wa hamoreru ka dō ka da yo! Deshō?
The most important thing about sex is coming together! Right?

When a man ejaculates more than once, there is a term popular with the red-light crowd specifying the exact number of orgasms experienced. *Nukani* refers to two orgasms, *nukasan*, to three, *nukayon*, to four, *nukago*, to five, and a super-human *nukaroku*, to six. All these terms are a contraction of *nukanai*, "not taking out," with any number as a suffix (*san*, "3," *yon*, "4," *go*, "5," etc.). The literal translation of a statement like *nukaroku* would read: "Without pulling out, I came six times in a row."

Ore sugē kōfun shite'ta kara nukasan shichatta yo!
I was so turned on that I came three times in a row!

Ima made no saikō kiroku wa ano onna to nukayon da yo.
My best record so far was with that woman when I came four times in a row.

P

PIN. Erection.

The most common slang terms for erection are:

> *Tatsu.* To stand.
> *Ō kiku naru.* To become big.
> *Genki ni naru.* To become lively.
> *Dekaku naru.* To become large.
> *Kataku naru.* To become hard.

Any of these expressions can be used in the following examples:

> *Ore no chimpo tatta!*
> My dick got hard!
> *Aitsu no asoko ōkiku natta!*
> His thing got hard!
> *Aitsu ikinari genki ni natta!*
> He suddenly got hard!

Pin is a sound word much like the English "boing," and is often used in conjunction with these terms to suggest the liveliness of the event and the immediacy of horniness.

> *Pin to ōkiku natta!*
> He suddenly got a rod on!
> *Pin to kataku natta!*
> He got rock hard!

The next step in *pin*'s slang evolution came when it broke loose from the other words for erection and became an idiom in its own right, useful for specifying a healthy, vibrant stiffness.

> *Ore no asoko sa, basu ni notte'ru to itsumo pin to natchimau!*
> You know, my dick always gets hard when I ride on busses!
> *Atashi kare ni yokkakatta no! Sō shitara aitsu ikinari pin to natte'n no!*
> I rubbed against him and he immediately got a rod on!

In schoolyards and on college campuses *pin* developed even further, becoming *Pinpin-chan*, "Mr. Boing Boing," a cute term for an erect penis, or for a young man's penis that is ready to rise at the drop of a hat.

> *Kare no pinpin-chan sugē kawain dakara.*
> I think his willy's cute when it gets hard.
> *Kare asa okiru to itsumo pinpin-chan ni natteru.*
> His pecker's always stiff in the morning.

Another term for vibrant erections, popular with the *bōsō-zoku* (motorcycle gangs) and other young Japanese motorcycle enthusiasts, is *uiri*, "wheelie," a word of American motorcyclist origin referring to the biker's precarious but flashy stunt of riding on the rear wheel only, with the front wheel raised off the ground.

> *Ano ko ga fuku o nuida totan, ore uiri shichatta!*
> The moment she took her clothes I got a rod on!

Another word for the erect male member enjoyed by the younger crowd is *kokachin*, believed to derive from *kōka*, "stiffening," and *chin*, "penis."

> *Omē kokachin'tte dore gurai ōkii no? Hakatta koto aru?*
> How big is your dick when it gets hard? Have you measured it?

A modern red-light district favorite for the erect male organ is *hakebune*, "sailing boat."

Atashi katai hakebune no otoko ga suki!
I like a man with a hard dick!

Cruder red-light words, used to intimate that the penis in question is startlingly large, are *gandaka* and *karidaka*. Both *gan* and *kari* are synonyms for "wild goose," *daka*, meaning "high" or "tall."

These words are seasoned *ingo* (criminal slang) expressions, used by people ranging from older hardened criminals to the younger street crowd that dotingly imitates their rough speech patterns.

Kinō sōpurando ni ittara, onna ga ore no gandaka massaji suru no umakute, ore sugu itchatta yo.
That chick at the Soapland massage place gave my stiff dick such a good workover that I came immediately.
Ore-tachi issho ni shawā abite'tara, Ken no yatsu karidaka ni natte'n no! Bukimi!
Us guys were taking a shower and Ken's dork got piss hard! It was weird!

If an erection occurs in the confines of one's trousers, manifesting itself in the form of a prominent bulge, the current slang term of choice would be *tento o haru*, "pitching a tent."*

Ano sutorippā ga dete kitara, ore sugu tento hatchimatta!
When that stripper came out, my pants bulged instantly!
Kawaisō na yatsu! Atashi no me no mae de tento hatte'ru no!
The poor bastard! Right in front of me his dick bulged in his pants!

---

* As a result of this tent motif it has become common, by extension, to refer to the penis as *tento mushi*, "tent bug," a pun on the word for "lady bird beetle."

R

REZU. Lesbian.

Japan has had a longstanding tradition of open-minedness when it comes to homosexuality—male homosexuality, that is. Lesbianism was never much of an issue, and although as Cherry Kittredge notes in her book *Womansword* "double dildos and other sex toys of preindustrial times speak irrefutably about the existence of lesbians," the interested historian will find little if any documented evidence of any pre-Meiji lesbian action. Sexual options were traditionally the privilege of men, who could either direct their sexual energy toward women or toward other men. Women had no sexual choices. Although Japanese lesbians have historically spoken only in subdued tones, the 1980s and 90s have brought louder statements—the first Japanese lesbian convention was held in 1985, new clubs and bars have opened nationwide, and new lesbian magazines have hit the scene. The formal term used in referring to lesbians is *rezubian*, which is preferred in lesbian circles to the more cumbersome native term *dōseiai no onna*, literally "same-sex-love-woman."

> *Ano hoteru de rezubian pātii aru kara, ikanai?*
> There's a lesbian party at that hotel, shall we go?

While *rezubian* is the formal term, the most common expression is the slightly derogatory contraction *rezu*, analogous to English words like "dyke," or "lez."

> *Atashi rezu yo! Dakara nan da 'tte yū no?*
> So I'm a dyke! You got a problem with that?

Parallel to the English slang trend that has turned the noun "dyke" into the verb "to dyke about," the Japanese have extended *rezu* into *rezuru*, which can either mean "to engage in lesbian sex" or "to act like a lesbian."

> *Rezutta koto aru?*
> Have you ever done it with another woman?
> *Mō sonna ni rezutte'naide yo! Hazukashii ja nai!*
> I wish you wouldn't act like such a dyke! It's so embarrassing!

In slangy speech *rezu* can also be made into an adjective: *rezu-ppoi*, "dyke-like," and *rezu-kusai* or the cruder *rezu-kusa*, meaning "stinking of dyke."

> *Sonna ni rezu-ppoi no yamete yo! Minna miru ja nai!*
> I wish you'd cut out acting like such a dyke! Everyone's looking!
> *Aa, 'ya da kono kamigata! Rezu-kusai yo!*
> Ooh, I hate this hairstyle! I look like some dyke!

A stronger expression, usually used to insult lesbians or large masculine-looking women, is *otoko-onna*, "man-woman."

> *Ano shingao no onna honto no otoko-onna da ne! Anta no koto jiro jiro miteru jan!*
> That new woman's a total bull dyke! She's like always looking at you!

One of the pejorative words for lesbian popular on the streets is *onabe*, "pan," a pun on the national Japanese insult for homosexuals, *okama*, "pot."

> *Ore zutto ano onna no koto dēto ni sasoitsuzukete'tan dakedo, tada no onabe dattan da yo!*
> I was trying to get her to go on a date with me, and it turns out she's a dyke!
> *Chotto anta, Suzuko onabe datta'tte shitte'ta?? Atashi sasowarechatta no!*

Did you know Suzuko was a lez?? She actually tried to pick me up!

Japanese street cliques, like their counterparts all over the world, are quick to crack down verbally, if not physically, on non-conformists. Lesbians are often favored targets for ribald criticisms. One of the seasoned insults is *chidori*, "the plover" or "wading bird," a favorite target for jokes in Japan because of its funny walk.

> *Atarimae jan! Chidori no ie itta yo! Ikura kureta to omou?*
> Of course I went with that dyke! You know how much she paid me?
> *Ano bā abunē yo! Chidori darake!*
> That bar's dangerous! It's fulla lesbos!

An even more offensive animal word favored in street-slang circles is *itachi*, weasel. In order to add muscle to a discriminatory remark about lesbians, the grammatical counters for animals are used instead of the counters for human beings: *rezu futari*, "two dykes," becomes *rezu nihiki*, "two dyke animals."

> *Ore ano nihiki no itachi dō yū fū ni yaru no ka! Shinjirarenē!*
> I can't imagine how those two bull bitches do it! Gross!

Another profound insult for lesbians is *gomora*, "Gomorrah," as in "Sodom and Gomorrah."

> *Aa! Atashi, anna gomora nanka kanojo wa suki nante shinjirannai!*
> Man! I can't believe she sees anything in a lesbo-slut like that!

A special slang word used in lesbian circles to specify the tough, masculine "dyke" is *otachi*, the Japanese equivalent of the American "bull dyke," or "diesel dyke." Like the male gay word *tachiyaku*, which is used for the tough "active" homosexual, *otachi* comes from the Kabuki theater, where *tachiyaku* designates the sturdy, dynamic masculine role.

Kanojo no gārufurendo'tte honto no otachi da mon ne.
Her girlfriend's a real bull dyke.
Suzuko wa otachi dakara, zettai doresu o kinai darō sā!
Suzuko's a bull-dyke, she'd never wear a dress!

The opposite of the strong, masculine-acting *otachi* is the feminine "femme" lesbian. The street-words for this type of lesbian were inspired, like *otachi*, by gay male slang, in this case *neko*, "cat," and *nenne*, "girly," both also synonyms for passive homosexuals.

Ano neko doko de hirotte kita no?
Where d'you pick that femme up?
Suzuko wa tsuyoi onna no koto suki ja nai no. Nenne ga suki nan da yo.
Suzuko's not into butch women, she likes femmes.

Some of the most insulting lesbian-related terms are the street words for lesbian sex. One of the favored terms is *kaiawase*, which would translate as "bumping pussy." *Kaiawase*, "meeting shells," is a traditional Japanese game in which shells are matched against each other. *Kai*, "shell," is also a street-slang word for vagina, giving *kaiawase* the additional meaning of "meeting vaginas."

Chotto uwasa ni yoru to, aitsu no okusan tonari no onna to kaiawase shite'ru rashii.
There are rumors that his wife's bumping pussy with the woman next door.
Kono bideo sugē kaiawase yatte'n no mieru ze!
This video shows some super cunt-grinding!

Even more potent than *kaiawase* is *ainame*, "mutual licking."

Atashi-tachi mō nagai aida ainame shiatte'run dakedo, saikō yo ne! Anta yattara ii no ni!
We've been going down on each other for years! It's great, you should try it!

RUMPEN. Destitute.

Some individuals cannot keep up with the fast-paced professional world of Japan. The loss of a job, followed by debts or
bankruptcy, and possibly with drugs, drink, and gambling
losses thrown in, can turn an affluent Tokyoite into a bum
living in the train station with a plastic bag or two. When this
happens, *rumpen*, a common slang term covering all types of
destitute and homeless people, is the word of choice.

The word *rumpen* arrived on the scene during the Taisho
period (1912–26), when the German political science term
Lumpenproletariat (shortened and pronounced *rumpen*) became
fashionable.

> *Aitsu rumpen mitai na kakko shite iru na.*
> That guy dresses like a bum.
> *Nande aitsu rumpen mitai ni narisagatchimattan da?*
> How come he ended up looking like such a bum?

While the word *rumpen* has enjoyed popularity with old and
young for over seventy years, recently the official term for
vagrant, *furōsha*, has been gaining popularity with the younger
generation.

> *Nan da kono furōsha darake!*
> Man! It's fulla bums here!
> *Kono furōsha kusē!*
> This bum stinks!

When a person does not make it in the fast-moving Japanese underworld and as a result lands on the street—going
from riches to rags—his former criminal colleagues might
choose the term *yasanuke*, "homeless," to describe him. This
ingo (criminal argot) word originated as *sayanuke*, "without a
sheath." *Saya* was inverted, as is the common practice of
Japanese street argot, to create *yasa*, today's standard sub-rosa
word for house.

> *Aitsu wa ima ja soto de yasanuke renchū to issho ni nete'run da ze.*
> He's ended up sleeping out in the open with a bunch of bums.
> *Nande ka shiranē kedo, aitsu yasanuke no hō ga suki mitai nan da yo na.*
> I dunno why, but it seems this guy prefers to be on the bum.

The same criminal crowd uses the analogous word *yasagure*, from *yasa*, "house," and *gureru*, "to go astray." This expression has two nuances: it can mean that the individual has fallen out of grace with society and ended up as a tramp, or it can refer to a man who has abandoned his house and family.

> *Asa kara ban made nomitsuzuke de, ano yasagure mō oshimae darō na!*
> That ragbag drinks from morning to night! He's finished!
> *Uchi no teishu totsuzen yasagure ni natchimatta no! Doko ikiyagattan da ka?*
> My old man just up and dumped me! I don't know where the fuck he went!

Another strong street word from Tokyo, reserved for those who have hit the skids after a life in the fast lane, is *gatakō*, "broken-down dude."

> *Kare wa sanjūgo da'tte yū no ni, miro yo anna gatakō ni natchatte!*
> He's just thirty-five and look how totally fucked up he is!
> *Aitsu sugē kanemochi nan da ze! Nande anna gatakō mitē na kakko suru no ka nē?*
> He's so rich! Why the hell does he dress like such a tramp?

Once these poor victims of society are down and out, the only ceiling they find over their heads, to quote an *ingo* (criminal slang) expression, is the *aokan*, "blue ceiling," the sky. *Aokan suru* or *aokan yaru*, "doing blue ceiling," implies sleeping in the open (which is illegal in Japan) because one has nowhere to go.*

> *Ano kōen ja minna sorotte aokan yatte'ru ze.*
> They all get together and sleep in the park.
> *Aitsu-ra doko ni mo iku toko ga nē kara, aokan suru shika nain da yo na!*
> They don't have no place to go, so they sleep outside!

The newest homeless problem in Japan is *Tokyo hōmuresu,* "Tokyo homeless," an expression coined as recently as the early 1990s. It refers to the masses of young people, who, arriving in Tokyo to study or look for work, find that they cannot make ends meet and end up sleeping on friends' couches, or at worst, doing *aokan,* "blue-ceiling."

> *Mō Tokyo hōmuresu bakkari yatte'rarenai kara, soro soro Utsunomiya ni kairanakya!*
> I've had enough of being without a place to stay! If this goes on I'm going back to Utsunomiya!
> *Tokyo no yachin'tte baka mitai ni takai kara, minna Tokyo hōmuresu ni natchau yo.*
> The rents here in Tokyo are so crazy that we're all gonna end up with no place to stay.

---

* *Aokan* has happier associations for the younger street crowd, for whom it means having sex in parks, on benches, and other places out in the open.

S

SENZURI. Masturbation.

The most common word for male masturbation in Japanese is *senzuri*, literally "a thousand rubs." It is essentially a slang expression analogous to the English "jerking off." Its long-standing popularity, however, has given it a semi-official standing, as indicated by its appearance in some of the progressive dictionaries. In its verb form it appears with the verbs *suru, yaru, kaku,* and *koku,* all meaning "to do" or "to perform."

> *Ore daitai ichinichi ni ikkai senzuri yaru yo.*
> I usually jerk off like once a day.
> *Atashi mada otoko ga senzuri suru no dō yaru ka wakannai.*
> I still don't get how guys jerk off.

Following the time-honoured Japanese gangster tradition of inverting words to make them incomprehensible to the casual bystander, *senzuri* was also reversed. The resulting *zurisen* has a rough, street-smart ring to it.

> *Ore mukashi, ie no ura de zurisen koite'ta toki mitsu-katchimatta koto arun da.*
> I was caught once beating off behind the house.
> *Omē konna zasshi de zurisen yatte'ru nante yūn ja nē yo! Kimochi warui!*
> Don't tell me you beat off looking at those magazines! Gross!

One of the official foreign words that has become very fashionable with the young is *masutabēshon,* "masturbation," followed by its somewhat less official truncated version, *sutabēshon*, "'sturbation."

> *Ore kinō masutabēshon no yarisugi de, chimpo ga itē ze!*
> I jerked off so much yesterday my dick's sore!
> *Aitsu no chinkoro chō-mikuro dakara, kitto yubi nihon de sutabēshon shichatte'ru!*
> His dick's so small I bet he jerks off with with just two fingers!

A popular expression throughout Japan, inspired by the first two syllables of "masturbation," is *masu*. It appears as a verb in the form *masu o kaku*, "stroking a *masu*." A funny little pun on *masu* that has recently appeared on the school scene is *Suma no ura*, "Suma backwards." The two syllables of Suma (a district in the western part of Kobe City) read "backwards" are *masu*.

> *Ore biichi ni iku to dōmo masu o kakitaku natchimaun da yo na.*
> Whenever I'm at the beach I get this urge to whack off.
> *Omae Suma no ura no toki donna ero fantajii miru?*
> What kinda fantasies do you have when you jerk off?

The official foreign word for masturbation is *onanii*, introduced by German medical tutelage during the 1870s. Over the years this initially decorous medical term has evolved a coarse aura that has kept it from entering polite conversation, and made it welcome on the street scene.

> *Kanojo no toshi ni natte mo mada onanii'tte suru no ka na?*
> I wonder if she still plays with it at her age!
> *Ore aniki ga heya de onanii shite'ru toko mitsukechatta!*
> I caught my brother jerking off in his room!

One of the native favorites for male masturbation is the melodious *shiko shiko*, "rub rub."

> *Nē, shiko shiko suru no'tte hada ni iin da'tte honto ka yo?*
> You think it's true that jerking off's good for the skin?

146

Otoko'tte jibun de shiko shiko suru no shinai furi surun da mon! Hen da yo ne!
Isn't it weird how guys always act like they never jerk off?

General terms for masturbation popular with both sexes are the more euphemistic *jibun de yaru*, "doing it on one's own," *hitori de yaru*, "doing it by oneself," and *hitorigokko*, "self-play."

Ammari jibun de yaru no'tte abunē ka na?
I wonder if it's bad for you to play with yourself too much!
Atashi hajimete hitori de yatta no wa, jūhachi no toki datta to omou!
The first time I played with myself was when I was eighteen!
Shinjirareru ka? Kagami o minagara hitorigokko surun da ze!
Do you believe this? He looks at himself in a mirror while he's playing with it!

Other general words for masturbation, used throughout Japan by all age groups, are *shigoki* and its verb form *shigoku*, "to stroke" or "squeeze a thing through one's hand."

Aitsu hen na yatsu da yo! Kondōmu kabusete shigoki su'n da'tte yo.
That dude's weird! He wears a condom to jerk off.
Ore shigoku no'tte ii to omou yo!
I kinda like jerking off!

A new word for masturbation popular among the new generation of Tokyo teenagers is *yamatesen*, "the Yamate Line." The Yamate Line is a Tokyo train line that goes around and around Tokyo in a nonstop circuit, which led the excitable brains of Japanese teenagers to draw a somewhat far-fetched parallel between the train's route and the actions of a masturbating hand. Another favorite with the same crowd is the more opaque *gōsuto raitā*, "ghost writer." The convoluted reasoning here is that *gōsuto* (ghost) implies secrecy (masturbation is almost invariably conducted in secrecy); the *raitā* (writer) "writes," which in Japanese (*kaku*) is a homophone for "stroking." So the ghost writer is the guy who "strokes in secret," or masturbates.

> *Motto wakai toki wa yoku yamatesen yatte'ta kedo, saikin wa mō yannai.*
> When I was younger I used to jerk off, but I don't anymore.
> *Ore dare no mae de mo zettai ni gōsuto raitā shinai!*
> I'd never jack off in front of anyone!

When an individual displays eccentricity in his or her masturbatory patterns, such as doing it in public, the action would be classified in street slang as *hen suru*, "doing the weird."

> *Hitomae de hen shita koto aru?*
> Did you ever play with yourself in front of anyone?
> *Ano kurabu wa tsumannē! Hen shika yatte nē!*
> That club's boring! All they do is beat off!

Some of the rougher words for masturbation come from the red-light district. Soapland massage parlors and other sex establishments offer what is known as *fingā sābisu*, "finger service," *fingā purē*, "finger play," and *fashon massāji*, "fashion massage," as part of their roster of masturbatory services. Some of these terms have spilled over into everyday street slang referring to self stimulation. Two such terms are *yubitsukai*, "using fingers," and *gonin gumi*, "the five-finger gang."

> *Kono oiru nan ni tsukau no? Aaa, yubitsukai no tame deshō?*
> What's that oil for? Oh, jerking off!
> *Ano otoko ore ga gonin gumi o suru no miru'ttsūnde nisen en haraiyagatte! Yatta!*
> That guy gave me fifteen bucks to watch me jerk off! Cool!

SHŌBEN. Urine.

The Japanese technical term for urine, *nyō*, is not used in everyday speech unless the speaker is talking about medical subjects like urine tests (*nyō kensa*) or diabetes (*tōnyōbyō*). The Japanese word that best parallels the English "urine" in nuance and texture is the traditional euphemism *shōben*, "small convenience" (its opposite *daiben*, "large convenience," is the euphemism of choice for "feces"). In everyday speech, however, *shōben* is superseded by its slangier variation *shomben*, which has the rough colloquial edge of English words like "piss" or "taking a leak," and is thus the *mot juste* in macho speech.

While the maturer man might still opt for the conventional *shōben*, even in rough informal speech, the younger crowd usually goes for *shomben*.

> *Omē! Tanomu kara! Michi de shōben shinai de kure yo na!*
> C'mon now! Please don't urinate in the street!
> *Chotto shomben itte kuru wa!*
> I'm just going for a quick leak!

A variation on *shomben* is *tachishomben*, "standing piss." This has two meanings: it refers to a man's standing pissing posture, and it is used as an idiom to specify that the pissing man is relieving himself not in a toilet but out in the open.

> *Otoko wa minna ano kado de tachishomben shite'ru!*
> The guys are all in that corner taking a leak!
> *Anta! Koko Tokyo nan dakara! Daremo tachishomben suru hito nanka nai wa yo!*
> C'mon, honey! This is Tokyo! People don't just piss in the street!

Another *shōben* word is *tsureshōben*, "pissing together." It started off as a village expression, used when people would take a break in their field work to go off together for a piss. Today people still quote the proverb *Inaka no tsureshōben*, "pissing together in the country." Unlike townspeople, Japanese villagers are very relaxed in matters concerning the body and its functions.

Nowadays *tsureshōben* is a sign of friendship and has become especially popular in schools and offices, where young girls often go off to the toilet in droves for a "wee-wee" and a chat. Teachers who watch their classes systematically empty out as the result of a severe case of *tsureshōben* might gruffly shout:

> *Tsureshōben yamenasai!*
> This going off for a piss together must stop!
> *Zen'in issho ni tsureshōben ikanaide hoshii!*
> Please don't all go at the same time!

Another *tsureshōben* proverb worth memorizing:

> *Tsureshōben, tabi no michi.*
> Pissing together on the road.

This proverb indicates that urinating together during an outing or a picnic is a sign of friendship. Ideally, close friends should be able to drop formalities and relax to the extent that even when nature calls they can respond in each other's company.

When it comes to urine there are words chiefly used by men (*shomben, tsureshomben*) and words predominantly used by women. Even though the technical term for urine, *nyō*, is not used in colloquial speech, it has played an important role by supplying Japanese slang with its urine-related vocabulary for women. The character for *nyō* (made up of the ideograms "tail" and "water") can also be read as *shito*, which developed into the dialect words *oshikko* and *shishi* (predominantly in the Harima region).* These words, being softer than *shomben*, have been taken up in everyday speech nationwide and are today the slang words for "piss" preferred by women. (Men will use

---

* *Nyō* and *shito* have been used in colloquial speech since pre-medieval times. Two memorable *shito* haiku are Yamazaki Sōkan's (1464–1552) mildy blasphemous:

oshikko when speaking to a woman, but would consider it effeminate to use among themselves).

> *Chotto matte'te! Umi ni haitte oshikko shite kuru kara!*
> Wait a minute! I'm going into the water to take a whizz!
> *Aa, mō, ki ni shinai! Mō kono kōen de shishi shichaē!*
> Oh, I don't care anymore! I'm gonna pee right here in the park!

Some provincial variations on *shomben* and *oshikko* that sound absolutely hilarious in Tokyo, and are thus used in jest, are *shombe*, from the Harima dialect, *shiko*, from the Jinji and the Kawachigun dialects, and *shiiko*, from the Tochigi dialect.

> *Chotto shitsurei! Ore shombe itte kimasu!*
> Would you please excuse me, I've got to go for a pish!
> *Wakai onna no ko wa soto de shiko nanka shimasen yo!*
> A young girl shouldn't piss outside!
> *Aa! 'Ya da! Kono ko mata pantsu ni shiiko shichatte!*
> Oh, no! The little brat pissed his pants again!

The Tokyo schoolyards, ever ready with witty new expressions, have recently come up with *jūroku*, "sixteen." (*Shishi*, meaning "piss," can also be interpreted as "four fours.")

> *Doa akecha dame! Ima obā-chan jūroku shite'ru kara!*
> Don't open the door! Granny's taking a leak!
> *Niwa de jūroku nanka shinaide! Itta deshō!*
> I've told you before, I wish you wouldn't piddle in the garden!

Saohime no	The goddess of spring
Harutachinagara	Standing
Shito o shite.	Takes a piss.

And Mastuo Bashō's (1644–94) earthy description of his stay in a desolate mountain hut:

Nomi shirami	Fleas, lice
Uma no shito suru	And a horse pissing
Makura moto.	By my pillow.

Another of the young generation favorites for "pissing" is the melodious *bibi*.

> *Toire ga kowaretchattara doko de bibi shitara iin darō?*
> If the toilet's broken where am I supposed to whizz?
> *Atashi anna pūru ni hairanai wa yo! Ittai nannin no hito ga naka de bibi shite'ru to omou?*
> I'm not going into that pool! Who knows how many people have pissed it?

A comic reference to a man's urinating is *tsutsuharai*. *Tsutsu*, "pipe," is a slang word for penis, and *harai* means to shake off. Thus *tsutsuharai* can also mean to shake off the penis after urinating.

> *Ore minna no mae de nanka, tsutsuharai dekinē!*
> I can't just piss in front of everyone!
> *Chan to tsutsuharai suru no wasurenaide yo!*
> Don't forget to shake off your thing after pissing!

One of the specialities of hard-core Japanese street slang is its collection of expressions dedicated to women urinating. Most of these terms capitalize on words suggestive of loud showerlike gushes. Two expressions that use natural phenomena to bring their point home are *gōu*, "downpour," and *yūdachi*, "sudden shower."

> *Aitsu-ra futari de issho ni gōu shi ni ita yo.*
> The two of them went to pop a squat.
> *Ano onna no yūdachi no oto ga sugokute, bā kauntā made kikoeta yo!*
> The sound of her pissing was so loud you could hear it all the way to the bar!

Two other red-light expressions for a woman's urinating are *teppō mizu*, "flash flood," and *manshon*. To the uninitiated Japanese ear, *manshon* means "apartment." This heavy slang expression did not originate from the English "mansion," but from *man*, "cunt," and *shon*, short for *shomben*, "piss."

Hanashi kakenaide yo! Ima teppō mizu no saichū nan dakara!
Don't talk to me now, I'm pissing like a race horse!
Chotto koko de matte'te! Atashi manshon shite kuru kara!
Wait for me here! I'm going to pop a squat!

SURI. Pickpocket.

Suri, the standard Japanese expression for pickpocket, was inspired by *suritsukeru*, "rubbing against," which is what your run-of-the-mill pickpocket does in busses, train stations, and especially the overcrowded rush-hour subways. To get pickpocketed in Japanese is expressed idiomatically as *suri ni au*, "encountering a pickpocket."

> *Kyō suri ni atte, tokei o torareta.*
> Some pickpocket swiped my watch today.
> *Chikatetsu ni nottara ki o tsukero yo! Suri darake dakara na!*
> Careful riding on the subway! It's fulla pickpockets!

The pickpockets are a strong and, by Western standards, well-organized group on the Japanese streets. They speak their own jargon, often unintelligible to outsiders, and have contributed a sizable vocabulary to mainstream criminal street slang, "the hidden language," *ingo*. One of the common insider terms on the streets for the pickpocket, inspired by his typical trait of constantly being on the lookout, is *ai-chan*, "Little Mr. Coincidence."

> *Onegai dakara, anna ai-chan renchū to tsukiau no wa yoshite yo!*
> I wish you wouldn't keep hanging out with that bunch of jostlers!
> *Aitsu ai-chan datta kedo ima ja yaku ni te dashite'ru.*
> He used to be a pickpocket, now he's dealing in drugs.

Another favorite term for pickpocket in the darker alleys of Tokyo is the provincial word *chibo*. Although it is not considered standard Japanese, its popularity in major dialects such as Kyoto, Osaka, Shikoku, Hiroshima, and Hokuriku has helped it gain a strong foothold on streets throughout Japan.

> *Nan da kono chibo! Ore no saifu ni te o dashiyagatte!*
> Man! That frisker laid his hands on my wallet!
> *Chibo yatte'ru no'tte omoshirē ze!*
> Being a frisker's fun!

Some of the "friskers," or "fingersmiths," as they are known on the American streets, are women. The Japanese lady pickpocket is known in street circles as *posuto*, "mailbox": anything she swipes gets stuffed down her blouse, like a letter into a mailbox.

> *Ano onna posuto datta! Ore no mono zembu totte nigeyagatta!*
> That woman was a pickpocket! She took all my stuff!
> *Ano posuto wa kao mo sugē kirei datta shi, teguchi mo kōmyō datta ze.*
> That girl pickpocket's not only good-looking, she works well too.

Belonging to the same group of pickpockets is the *wappa hazushi*, who specializes in snatching rings and bracelets off his victim's hands. This *ingo* criminal slang term is made up of *wappa*, "ring" or "bracelet," and *hazusu*, "to unfasten."

> *Ano wappa hazushi honto ni kurōto da ze! Aitsu no shigoto mita koto aru kai?*
> That ring thief's a real pro! Have you seen him work?
> *Aitsu-ra wappa hazushi tsukamaeyō to shitan dakedo, nigerarechimatta.*
> They tried catching that ring swiper but he got away.

A related type of street criminal is the *oihagi*, from *oi*, "to follow," and *hagi*, "stripping off." The *oihagi* started his career in old Japan as a highwayman, following, catching, and stripping hapless travelers of their belongings. On today's Japanese streets he has been transmogrified into a purse snatcher.

154

Oihagi ga ushiro kara kite, atashi no baggu hittakutte ita.
That purse snatcher came up behind me and grabbed my bag.
Zettai ni atashi no mono totte itta oihagi mitsukerarenai to omou na!
I'm sure they'll never find that purse snatcher who took all my things!

The victim or "target" of any of the above thieves is known in *ingo* slang as *gaisha*, short for *higaisha*, "victim," or rather sardonically as *kyaku*, "customer."

Kyō wa nannin no gaisha ni atattan dai?
How many scores didja do today?
Ichiban ii kyaku'tte no wa, chikatetsu no naka no yatsu darō na.
The best easy marks, I guess, are the ones in the subway.

When pickpocket specialists convene for in-depth conversation, outsiders, even if they are criminals of a different persuasion, find it difficult to fathom what is being said. Every method and hand movement involved in pickpocketing has a specialized terminology, not to mention the insider words for all the objects stolen.

Thus *uguisu*, a small songbird favored in traditional Japanese poetry, takes on the meaning of "gold watch." "Ring," known in standard Japanese as *yubiwa*, "finger ring," is inverted in pickpocket slang, resulting in *wayubi*, or transformed into *waibi*, or *guruwa*, "round-ring." The wallet is known as *iwa*, or "rock," and the empty wallet *iwagara*, "rock-empty"; if an individual takes the money and then throws the wallet away, the term of choice would be *iwagaracharu*, "rock-emptying."

Some of the key Japanese pickpocket words are the names of the different pockets that the coveted wallet might be in. The back pocket, or "ass pocket" is known as *shiriba*, "ass place"; an outside pocket is known as *sotoba*, "outside place," and the harder-to-get-at inside pocket is the *uchiba*, "inside place."

155

Ano otoko iwa o shiriba ni ireteta kara raku datta ze.

That guy had his wallet in his back pocket, so it was a pushover.

Ichiban yariyasui gaisha wa yappa' sotoba ni kane irete'ru toshiyori da yo na!

The easiest targets are those old idiots who carry their money in their outside pockets!

Ore ga ima neratta yatsu, uchiba datta kara yarinikukatta ze!

The guy I just did was tough! It was in his inside pocket!

T

TE GA HAYAI. Fast worker.

A lady-killer with a smooth-talking and fast-working technique is applauded by his peers with the phrase *te ga hayai*, "the hands are quick," or just *hayai*, "quick," for short.

On Japanese streets quick-handed lady-killing is admired, and the "wolf" or the "make-out artist," as he is known in America, stands in high regard with his colleagues. While most English synonyms for lady-killer harbor an undertone of respect, the Japanese equivalents tend to be perceived in general speech as insults.

> *Ken no yarō'tte! Honto ni te ga hayai ze! Sugu onna hikkakete kuru!*
> Ken's a real ruthless bastard! He just picks up one women after the other!
> *Omae sore'tte hayai ze! Ikkai dēto shita dake de mō beddoin ka yo!*
> Man! You're fierce! You laid her after just one date!

A slangy but popular expression for an attractive young man is *iro otoko*, "sexy man." It originated in medieval Japan, where *iro no machi*, "the city of sex," was one of the names for the red-light district. The *iro otoko* in those days were the men who either worked or frequented "the city of sex." What started out as an offensive expression has today turned into a compliment analogous to English expressions like "stud" and "hunk."

> *Ii jan, ano iro otoko! Nani mono, moderu?*
> Ooh, what a hunk! What is he, some kinda model?

Anta to dēto shita iro otoko, dare yo?
Who was that stud you were going out with?

The lady-killer or playboy is known derogatorily as *onna-tarashi*, literally "woman-deceiver." The younger generation version is the abbreviated *tarashi*.

Anta'tte honto ni onnatarashi ne! Anta nanka kirai yo!
You're always playing around with other girls! I hate you!
Atashi anna tarashi nanka ni chikazukanai wa!
I'm not getting involved with such a heartless playboy!

One of today's teenage expressions used in discussing smooth-talking pretty boys is *ama-chan*, "little Mr. Sweet."

Ki o tsukenakya dame yo! Ano ama-chan abunai kara!
You'd better be careful, girl! That little wolf's dangerous!
Ne! Kondo no shin'iri amachan tondemonaku kakkō yoku nai? Tabetai!
That smooth new kid's real sharp! I'm gonna snatch him up!

Another highly fashionable school-slang expression for the ruthless playboy is *eitoman*, "eight man." This was inspired by the comics character *eitoman*, who has eight different faces that he can put on at will, much like the two-timing, or in this case "eight-timing" little playboy, who has a different act for every girl he dates.

Moshi kare eitoman yamenain dattara, anna yatsu wakareru yo!
If he's not gonna quit messing around I'm gonna dump him!
Ii ko butte'ru kedō, ano otoko'tte honto no eitoman da yo ne!
He acts all innocent, but he's a total killer!

Another type of smooth operator is the *madamu kirā*, literally "the madam-killer," a Japanese variation on the English "lady-killer." This expression of the younger generation has two meanings: it is used for an attractive young man who is *te ga hayai,* "quick-handed," and goes through women with breath-taking speed. It also has a newer meaning that comes from the college campuses, where there is a growing phenomenon of attractive but poor male students who act as boyfriends to wealthy middle-aged women. A variation on this neologism is *obatarian kirā. Obatarian* is a vicious popular insult for the middle-aged woman (from *oba,* "old woman," and *batarian,* the Japanese pronunciation of "battalion," which was the title of a horror movie that hit Tokyo in the late 1980s about a battalion of flesh-eating zombies from outer space).

> *Uchi no daigaku'tte madamu kirā darake da yo ne!*
> My university's teeming with candy-boys!
> *Shiranakatta no? Ken no shōtai wa sugoi obatarian kirā wa yo!*
> You mean you didn't know? Ken's actually a gigolo for all those old broads!

U

UNKO. Shit.

To translate the exact nuance of *unko* into English one would need an expression midway between an earthy "shit" and a more playful "poot." It is this dichotomy of the vulgar and the cute that makes *unko* Japan's favorite expression for chatting casually about feces.

Unko's etymology is much disputed among Japanologists. One theory is that *un* is an imitation of the deep-throated grunt sometimes discharged during an arduous bout of defecation, while *ko*, the diminutive suffix, gives the word its euphemistic texture. A more formalistic school of thought asserts that this expression was inspired by the Japanese hiragana syllabary: the first syllable, *a*, symbolizing food entering the mouth, the last syllable *un*, representing food departing from the anus. Although *unko* is a slang word, its universal popularity endears it to respectable grannies as much as to the not-so-respectable criminal elements.

> *Ken wa toire de unko shite'ru no.*
> Ken's taking a shit in the toilet.
> *Chotto unko ga shitai kara, koko de matte'te!*
> Wait for me here, I have to go for a quick shit!

To give *unko* extra slangy "oomph," speakers sometimes opt for the juicier *bakuon unko*, "explosive shit."

> *Aa! Yatto ma ni atta ze! Nante bakuon unko darō!*
> Man, I made it just in time! That was quite a dump I took there!

161

> *Ano ko resutoran de sugē bakuon unko suru kara, minna taberu no yametchatta ja nai yo!*
> At the restaurant she took such a loud shit everyone like stopped eating!

One version of *unko* that is thought to be more *kawaii*, "cute," is *unchi*, whose childlike playfulness makes it a favorite among the girls.

> *Aa! Gomen! Atashi unchi shita kara ima hairu to kusai yo!*
> Woops! Don't go in there now! I just took a shit, so it stinks!
> *'Ya da atashi! Konna soto de unchi dekinai wa yo!*
> No way! I can't just take a shit out here!

A nasty new slang word for "squat," inspired by *unchi*, is *unchingu sutairu*, "shitting style," an Anglo-Japanese expression that was created by adding *-ingu*, as in shit*ting*, to *unchi*, shit," with *sutairu*, the English word "style," stuck on. An even rougher version, *unkozuwari*, "shit sitting," is favored by the younger street crowd.

> *Sonna unchingu sutairu de suwaranaide!*
> Don't squat as if you were taking a shit!
> *Nan de aitsu-ra unkozuwari de basu matte yagaru? Koko inaka ja nai yo!*
> Why are these guys squatting in such a disgusting way at that bus stop? It's not like we're in some field!

A playful variation on *unko* is the dialect word *onkobo*, a term originally from the Chōzu dialect. It is considered side-splittingly funny in Tokyo, where the in-crowd is constantly on the prowl for the most *dasai*—un-cool—sounding provincial words. These words are picked up and used as facetiously as possible, often followed by raucous peals of laughter, at the expense of those less elegant in speech.

> *Dare ga niwa ni onkobo shita no ka ne?*
> All right! Who dropped a turd in the garden?

Aa warui kedo, onkobo ni ikitai!
Sorry, but I have to drop a log!

The other key slang word for "shit" in Japanese is *kuso*. The character for *kuso* is made up of two components: "tail" on top and "rice" on the bottom, and is closely related to the character for *nyō*, "urine," which is made up of "tail" on top and "water" on the bottom. *Kuso* is as widely used as *unchi* but has a slightly rougher quality. It is similar to the English "shit" in that besides its literal reference to feces it is also used as an expletive indicating rage or frustration. *Kuso!* can be translated as "Shit!," "Damn!," or "Fuck!" It can also be used as an emphatic prefix: *kuso-baba*, "fuckin' bitch," or *kuso-kuruma*, "fuckin' car."

Toire wa doko da? Ore kuso ga shitē!
Where's the toilet? I've to go for a crap!
Onegai dakara! Kuso shita ato nagasu no wasurenaide kure yo!
Please! I wish you wouldn't forget to flush after you take a shit!

When defecation takes place out in the open, like in a garden, park, or on the sidewalk, a popular slang term is *noguso*, "field shit," which was originally used in the strict sense of defecating out in the fields, away from one's hut. Nowadays, due to widespread urbanization, *noguso* has become more ductile in meaning.

Anta noguso shinaide yo! Koko Tokyo dakara! Saitama ja nai yo!
I wish you wouldn't shit outside! This is Tokyo, not Saitama!*
Minna ga mite'ru no ni noguso nanka dekinai yo!
I can't take a shit out here with everyone watching!

---

* Saitama, which is right outside Tokyo, has been traditionally used by Tokyoites as the ultimate symbol of provinciality.

A punny street-slang variant on *kuso* is *kyū-jū*, "nine-ten." The link between these numerals and feces is that the characters for "nine" and "ten" usually read *kyū* and *jū*, can also be read as *ku* and *so*. In the rare case that this variant is actually put in writing, like on the wall of a public toilet, it will appear either in the characters for "nine" and "ten," or—the ultimate in radicality—the numerals "9/10."

> *Kuruma tomete kurenai? Chotto kyūjū ga shitain da yo ne!*
> Can you stop the car? I just wanna drop a quick turd!
> *Babā ga kyūjū shita ato'tte doko mo kashiko mo kusakute tamannē!*
> When the old woman takes a crap the whole place stinks sky-high!

A colorful but somewhat coarse synonym for defecating popular among the younger generation is *mori mori suru*. The term *mori mori* is in itself a harmless adverb suggesting intense activity: *mori mori kū*, "to eat like crazy," or *mori mori benkyō suru*, "to study like crazy." But the reason teenagers saw *mori mori* as a prime candidate for a feisty analogy for shit is that when used alone it evokes a sense of rapid piling up.

> *Uchi no otōto ima mori mori shite'ru kara, haitcha dame yo!*
> My brother's dumping in there, don't go in!
> *Chotto kami chōdai! Atashi mori mori ni ikitai no yo.*
> Give me some paper, I have to take a dump.

When one specifically wishes to discuss a piece of shit, as opposed to the act of defecating itself, street-slang terms used by the young would be *toguro*, "coil," and more general expressions like *ōkii no*, "a big one," or *ōkii yatsu*, "a large guy."

> *Mō toire ni sugoi toguro ga atta yo! Dare ga yatta no?*
> There's a big turd in the toilet! Who did it?
> *Obā-chan! Ōkii no ga deta yo!*
> Grandma! I did a big one!

Komatta na! Toire ga nai nante! Ore ōkii yatsu shitēn da yo!
Damn! There's no toilet around here! I've gotta dump a
load!

Devotees of sexual games involving defecation indulge in
what is known in Japan as *unko purē*, "shit play," an expression
that originated in the red-light areas.

*Suimasen! Chotto okiki shitain desu keredomo! Donna unko
purē yatte'run desu ka?*
Excuse me! What type of "brown games" do you offer
here?
*Anna otoko suteta wa yo! Datte, unko purē shitai nante yūn
da mon!*
I split up with him! He like wanted me to do "brown"
stuff!

Another sexual penchant related to bowel movement is the
enema, known to Japanese enthusiasts as *ero kanchō*, "erotic
enema," or *kanchō purē*, "enema play."

*Kare nannen mo atashi ni ero kanchō shitsuzukete'ru wa!
Sugoku kōfun surun dakara!*
He's been giving me enemas for years! It still turns him
on like crazy!
*Na! Ano Ikebukuro no kurabu de kanchō purē yatte'ru'tte,
honto ka?*
Hey! Is it true they do enemas at that Ikebukuro club?

W

WANPATAN. Boring.

Wanpatan (with the stress on the first and last *a*) belongs to the growing body of "made in Japan" English expressions. These fashionable words are known as *waseigo*, "Japan-made-language," and they are created when Western words or phrases, usually English, are modified, redefined, and then absorbed into everyday speech.*

Wanpatan is the Japanese pronunciation of "one pattern," which is, from a logical standpoint, the perfect synonym for "boring." In modern Japanese, parties, people, books, food, or anything can be labeled *wanpatan*.

> *Kare-ra no pātii wa itsumo wanpatan da yo! Zurakare!*
> Their parties are always so boring! Let's split!
> *Kare'tte itsumo wanpatan na gyagu shika iwanain da mon! Saitei!*
> His jokes are *so* stale! The worst!

In Tokyo schoolyards, witty youngsters have engendered the zaniest analogies for the word "boring" that the Japanese language can boast. The basis of these clever neologisms is the semantic reinterpretation of *wanpatan*, which these creative youngsters dissolved into *wan*, "woof," as in "bark," and *patan*, "bang." The resulting expression is the hilarious *koketa inu*,

---

* *Waseigo* words range from ordinary expressions like *poketto beru*, "pocket bell," for "beeper," and *uerunessu dorinku*, "wellness drink," for "sports shake," to more risqué terms like *daburu purē*, "double play," for "fellatio," or *sukuryū*, "screw," for "penis."

"the stumbling dog." (When the poor animal stumbles, one is likely to hear a woof followed by a bang).

> *Kyō no miitingu mata koketa inu!*
> Today's meeting was so *boring!*
> *Eikaiwa no kurasu ikitaku nai wa! Dōse koketa inu nan dakara!*
> I don't wanna go to my English class! It's such a drag!

Another droll synonym for "boring" that sprang from the "woof-bang" school is *inu no soto*, "the dog outside," the concept here being that the dog went "woof," the door went "bang," and—*Wan!! Patan!!*—the dog was shut out.

> *Atashi yoku ano disuko ni itte'ta kedō, ima mō inu no soto da mon nē!*
> I used to go to that club all the time, but it's got like totally dull!
> *Aitsu jibun de wa omoshiroi to omotte'n da ze! Tada no inu no soto no kuse shite yo!*
> He thinks he's so cool, but he's such a major yawn!

Other Japanese teenage neologisms for "boring" come from the musical world. An individual who is irritatingly predictable in speech, thought, and action, a "pain in the ass" as an American would say, would be branded by high-school cliques as a *kasetto ningen*, "cassette-tape human," who, like a tape, becomes boring and predictable after constant replay.

> *Omae kasetto ningen jan!*
> You're a real pain in the ass!
> *Aitsu mainichi umi ni ikitagaru yo! Tada no kasetto ningen jan!*
> He's so predictable! All he's interested in is going to the beach!

Closely related to *kasetto ningen* is the new teenage slang expression *endoressu ningen*, "endless human" (from the idea of endless-play casette tapes), and more recently just *endoressu*, for short (the English word "endless").

Mō konna tsumannē hanashi kikitaku nē yo! Aitsu honto endoressu ningen da!

I don't wanna hear all that boring crap! He's such a total pain in the ass!

Omae'tte endoressu da yo na! Ore kaeru yo!

You're such a fuckin' drag! I'm leaving!

Y

YARU. To do in.

Yaru, literally "to do," is one of the older and more vicious Japanese underworld expressions for killing. It has been a longtime criminal expression in Japan that, like its American equivalent, "doing someone in," has become a favorite since it was taken up by the Yakuza movies of 1950s and '60s.

> *Aitsu o yare!*
> Let's do him in!
> *Aitsu o yatta!*
> I bumped him off!

The standard Japanese word for killing or murdering is *korosu*. It is a powerful and negative word; its character, which can also be read as *satsu*, appears in many lethal terms: *koroshi*, "killing," *koroshiya*, "hired killer," *satsu batsu to shita*, "brutal," *satsugai*, "slaying," *satsujin*, "homicide," *satsujin hannin*, "murderer," *jisatsu*, "suicide," and *satsuriku*, "massacre." This scary character is made up of the two elements "pig," and "smite," the idea being the killing of a pig. By the time the term was shipped to Japan, its meaning had already shifted to imply killing in general. For a fiercer and slangier edge the prefix *bu* is added, resulting in *bukkorosu*, "totally kill." *Korosu* and *bukkorosu* can also be used idiomatically to mean "beating the shit out of."

> *Omē kane harawanē nara, korosu ze!*
> I'll kill you if you don't hand over the cash!

Aitsu, satsu ni tarekondari shitara bukkoroshite yaru!
If he squeals to the cops we'll fuckin' kill him!

Beyond the familiar expressions *yaru* and *korosu* there exists a whole roster of street words involving killing and death that are still cherished among the criminal *ingo* (hidden language) speakers but have never been launched by the media into mainstream speech. One of these is *mageru*, "to twist" or "to bend."

Dare ga ano jiji magetan da yo? Omē-ra?
Who killed that old dude? Was it you guys?
Ore-tachi hikkoshita ze! Magerarechimau mon na!
We moved outa there! We were gonna get killed!

Another oldtimer on the *ingo* slang-scene is *shimeru*, literally "to close."

Ano baba aitsu-ra ni shimerareta ze! Shirisugite'ta kara na!
They finished that bitch off! She knew too much!
Ano renchū ittai nannin shimetan da? Kono futari dake?
How many guys did that group wipe out? Only those two?

On the same *ingo* slang wordlist is *tomeru*, "to stop."

Kotoshi no rokugatsu, aitsu-ra uchi no jiji o tometa!
Last June they bumped off my old man!
Ano yarō ki ni sawarun dattara, tometchimae yo!
If he gets in the way, kill him!

Another rough criminal slang term used to chat about killing people is *tatamu*, "to fold."

Aitsu-ra ano otoko o tatande kawa ni nagesuteta!
They finished him off and threw him in the river!
Aitsu tatanjimaō ze! Kane wa yamawake da!
Let's finish him off and split the cash!

A vicious euphemism for murder popular among the criminal crowd is *nesaseru*, "to put to sleep."

Aitsu nesaseta ato, karada wa dō surun no yo?

What am I supposed to do with his body after I've finished him off?

Ano renchū ima keimusho ni haitte'ru! Nannin ka nesasechimatta kara na!

That bunch is in prison now! Who knows how may people they've bumped off!

In the same group of hard-line streetwords for murder is *chirasu*, "to scatter."

Dare ano chiraseta onna? Omae shitte'ru?

Who's that woman they got rid of ?

Ore daremo chirasanē ze! Jōdan ja nē yo!

No way man! I'm not doing no killing!

REFERENCES

Asano, Kenji. *Sendai Hōgen Jiten*. Tokyo: Tōkyōdō Shuppan, 1985.

Chapman, Robert. *American Slang*. New York: Harper & Row, 1987.

Daigo, Yoshiyasu. Kenko Kotowaza Jiten. Tokyo: Tōkyōdō Shuppan, 1985.

Dickson, Paul. *Slang!* New York: Harper Collins, 1990.

Gendai Yōgo No Kiso Chishiki. Tokyo: Jiyū Kokuminsha, 1990.

Ino, Kenji. *Gendai Wakamono Kotoba Jiten*. Tokyo: Nihon Keizai Hyōronsha, 1988.

Inokuchi, Yūichi. *Kyōtogo Jiten*. Tokyo: Tōkyōdō Shuppan, 1975.

Kabashima, Tadao. *Meiji Taishō Shingo Zokugo Jiten*. Tokyo: Tōkyōdō Shuppan, 1984.

Lewin, Esther. *The Random House Thesaurus of Slang*. New York: Random House, 1988.

Makimura, Shiyō. *Ōsaka Kotoba Jiten*. Tokyo: Kōdansha, 1985.

Matsumoto, Takio. *Harima Hōgen Shūtetsu*. Tokyo: Taiyō Shuppan, 1983.

Miyoshi, Ikkō. *Edogo Jiten*. Tokyo: Tokyo Seiabō, 1971.

Morishita, Kiichi. *Tochigi-ken Hōgen Jiten*. Tokyo: Tōkyōdō Shupann, 1975.

Park, Whaja. *Aspects Contrastifs Du Japonais Et Du Coreen*. Stockholm: Stockholm University, 1982.

____. *Western Loanwords In Japanese*. Stockholm: Stockholm University, 1982.

Rawson, Hugh. *A Dictionary of Euphemisms & Other Double Talk*. New York: Crown Publishers Inc., 1981.

Sema, Takashi. *Kaigun Yōgo Omoshiro Jiten*. Tokyo: Kojinsha 1983.

Shibatani, Masayoshi. The Languages of Japan. Cambridge: Cambridge University Press, 1990.

Yamanaka, Jōta. *Hōgen Zokugo Gogen Jiten*. Tokyo: Kōsō Shobō, 1970.

Yoshizaki, Junji. *Jisho ni nai Kotoba no Jiten*. Tokyo: Nihon Bungeisha, 1986.

JAPANESE WORD LIST

Abazure, 87–88
Aburauri, 29–30
Agari, 50
Ahen, 101
Ahenchū, 102
Ahen jōyōsha, 102
Ahen kutsu, 102
Ahen kyūinjō, 102
Ahen Torishimari Hō, 101
Aho, 8–9
Ahondara, 9
Ai, 3
Ai-chan, 153
Aijin, 4
Ainame, 140
Aki, 50
Akinaishi, 50
Akisu, 50
Akuse jarajara, 100
Ama-chan, 158
Ambako, 91
Ampontan, 10–11
Anaru sekkusu, 25
Anatsutai, 50
Anko, 48
Aokan, 142–43
Ā-pā gyaru, 57
Ara, 55
Are, 6
Asarifumi, 50
Ashi-kun, 76–77
Ashiname-ma, 20
Aashindo, xvi

Asoko, 6, 20, 24–25, 105,
    131, 133, 134
Atama, 12
Atarabachi, 71
Ate, 55
Ateire, 105

Baba (babā), xv, 36, 172
Bairin gyaru, 57
Baishun assen gyōsha, 71
Baishunfu, 36
Baita, 88
Bājin, 37
Baka, 7–8, 21
Baka-chin, 8
Baka-mono, 8
Baka ni suru, 48
Baka yarō, 7, 48, 91
Bakuon unko, 160–61
Banchō, 12
Banchoppari, 26
Bebe, 129
Beddoin, 157
Benri-kun, 76–77
Berusasa gyaru, 57
Bibi, 152
Bi-ei, xv
Bimbā, 81–82
Bimbesuto, 81–82
Bimbō, 81–82
Bitamin esu, 41
Bobo, 104, 128–29
Bobowaru, 104
Bōifurendo, 5, 105

Bōsōzoku, 11–12, 134
Bū, 15–16
Būbū, 12–13
Buchikorosu, 47
Bukimi, 135
Bukkomu, 69–70
Bukkorosu, 119, 171
Buppanasu, 33
Busu, 14, 114
Būsuka, 13
Busukureru, 114
Butabako, 91
Būtareru, 114
Butsu, 66, 67
Buttobu, 108

Champon, 17
Charamporan, 17–18
Chibo, 154
Chichi, 18–19
Chichi kurushii, 19
Chidori, 139
Chijo, 20
Chikan, 19–20
Chikuri-ma, 20
Chikushō, 21, 116
Chimpira, 21–22
Chimpo, 22, 23, 24, 69, 133, 146
Chimpoko, 23
Chimpoko no atama, 23
Chinchin, 23–24
Chinko, 23
Chinkoro, 146
Chirasu, 173
Chirō, 24–25
Chitsu, 25
Chō-etchi, 37
Choko, 108
Chomboru, 120
Chonga, 26–27
Chūshaki, 66

Daburu etchi, 37
Daisuki, 3, 39, 43
Damare, 8, 91
Dan gū, 54
Dani, 29
Danidachi, 29
Dankon, 30
Darashinai onna, 31
Dasu, 32–33
Debu, 33, 114, 124
Deburu, 33
Debusen (zoku), 34
Deka, 34–35
Dekachin, 24
Dekaku naru, 133
Dekigokoro, 121
Dekoru, 35
Dembu, 93
Dendokokeshi, 68
Deru, 32
Dii rain, 117
Do-eirian, 15
Do-etchi, 37
Do-kechi, 89
Dorobō, 119
Dōseiai no onna, 137
Do-tsubo, 115

Efu emu, 5
Eichi bii, 14
Ēei eichi ō, 9
Eirian, 15
Eitoman, 158
Ekisutora etchi, 37–38
Emma, 55
Emu, 38–39
Emu-teki, 38–39
Endoressu ningen, 168–69
Enyon, 26
Ero, 39–40
Ero-bide, 39
Erochika, 40

Erochikku, 39
Ero den, 39
Ero fantaji, 39, 146
Ero hon, 39
Eroi, 39
Ero kanchō, 20, 39, 163
Ero kasseto, 39
Ero shashin, 39
Esu, xv, 40–42, 116
Esu efu, 5
Etchi, 37–38
Etchi suru, 38

Fashon massji, 148
Faundēshon jiwa, 36
Fera, 43
Ferachio, 43
Fing purē, 148
Fingā sābisu, 148
Fukuchon, 27
Fummatsu, 66
Furōsha, 141
Furuchin, 24
Furūto, 44
Futanari, 126
Futotta, 117

Gacha, 34
Gaijin no suke, 99
Gaisha, 155
Gametsui, 89–90
Gandaka, 135
Garasuhazushi, 51
Garikamaru, 118
Gārufurendo, 5, 140
Gatakō, 142
Gatsu gatsu, 90
Gei, 45
Gei boi, 45
Gei boi san, 45
Gei-chikku, 46
Gejashiku, 27

Genkin, 46
Genki ni naru, 133
Gennama, 46–47
Gero, 83
Gero gero, 83
Gin gin, 6, 30, 69
Giru, 121–22
Gobō, 48
Gobō no kiriguchi, 95
Goji made gyaru, 57
Gōkan-ma, 20
Gokusaishiki, 35–36
Gomora, 139
Gonin gumi, 148
Gōsuto raitā, 148
Go taimu, xv
Gōtō, 49–50
Gōu, 152
Gū, 53–54
Gudō, 55
Gui, 51
Guruwa, 155
Gyaru, 57–59
Gyaru bōi, 58
Gyaruo-kun, 58
Gyaru otoko, 59
Gyaru oyaji, 59

Hadejara, 99–100
Hādo gei, 46
Hādo koa, 46, 125
Hai, 100, 107
Hai nashi, 79
Hajiki, 55
Hakebune, 134
Hakike, 14
Hako, 70
Hako yari, 70
Hamekomu, 68–69
Hameru, 68
Hamoru, 132
Happa, 107–8

Happaboke, 108–9
Happachū, 108–9
Haraboji, 27
Harabote, 117–118
Haramu, 115–16
Hawai san, 108
Hayai, 156
He, 61–63
Hei beibi, 95
Heitai, 12
Hekoki, 62
Hen suru, 148
Hero, 64
Herochū, 67
Heroin, 64
Heroin chūdoku kanja, 67
Herokan, 67
Hero kutsu, 68
Hetare, 62
Hibotsuki, 72
Higo, 47
Himo, 29, 71–72, 115
Himotsuki, 72
Hine daikon, 31, 49
Hinkuya, 80
Hinkuya-mitai, 80
Hinkuya-ppoi, 80
Hinkuyaru, 80
Hirogeru onna, 32
Hiropon, 74–75
Hitori de yaru, 147
Hitorigokko, 147
Hitouchi, 68
Hōhi, 61
Hoken otoko, 77–78
Hommei-kun, 76
Homo, 45
Hosuto genshō, 78
Hoteru, 92

Ichimaimono, 51
Ichimon nashi, 79

Ii jan, *xvii*
Ijiri-makuri-mawasu, 106
Ijirimakuru, 106
Ijirimawasu, 106
Ijiru, 30, 105–6
Ikasu, 54
Iku, 32, 41, 111
Imaichi (ni, san, hyaku, sen, jūman), 82
Imo, 49, 83–84
Imobē-da, 84
Imochi, 84
Imo-chikku, 84–85
Imo-kusai, 84–85
Imo nēchan, 83–84
Imo-ppoi, 84–85
Imo yarō, 83
Imozoku, 84
Inaori, 51
Indo san, 108
Inharabebii, 116–17
Inkyo, 92
Inu no soto, 168
In'ya, 34
Irau, 105
Irekomu, 71
Iri, 51
Iro otoko, 157
Irou, 105
Itabakasegi, 51
Itabashiri, 51
Itachi, 139
Itafumi, 51
Itanomikasegi, 51
Ite, 34
Iwa, 155–56
Iwagacharu, 155–56
Iwagaru, 155–56

Jibun de yaru, 147
Jii, 65–66
Jiji, 89, 99, 172

Jimijara, 100
Jinkoro, 34
Jorō, 87
Joseiki, 25
Junnama, 111
Jūroku, 151
Kagu, 64
Kai, 140
Kaiawase, 140
Kaikuri, 51
Kaimono suru, 121
Kajidoro, 51
Kakkoii, 54, 77
Kakuseizai, 75
Kame, xvi
Kane, 29, 62, 73, 79, 80, 87,
  90, 120, 122, 156
Kanebako, 51
Kanejū, 56
Kanekuchi, 52
Kanetataki, 52
Kamisori-ma, 20
Kanchō-ma, 20
Kancho purē, 163
Kangoku, 90
Kani, 56
Kankin, 91
Kanko, 129
Kanojo, 4–5, 15, 16, 55, 126
Kapparau, 119
Kare, 4–5, 16, 38, 81
Karidaka, 135
Kasetto ningen, 166
Kataku naru, 6, 133
Kau, 121
Kebai, 99
Kebajara, 99–100
Kebakebashii, 98
Kechi, 89–90
Kechi-kusai, 89
Kechimbō, 89
Keimusho, 22, 90–92, 173

Kemanjū, 25–26
Kerikomi, 52
Ketsu, 93–95
Ketsumedo, 95
Ketsu no ana, 94
Ketsu no ana de yaru, 94
Ketsu-nuke, 11
Kikuza, 95
Kimatte'ru, 54
Kimpatsu, 31, 35
Kinketsubyō, 81
Kintama, 95–96
Kiipu-kun, 76
Kiza, 97–98
Kizaru, 98n
Kōchisho, 91
Kōgan, 95
Koibito, 4
Kokachin, 134
Koketa inu, 167–68
Kokku sakkingu, 44
Kokku sakkingu gēmu, 44
Kokku sakkingu purē, 44
Kona, 65
Kondōmu, 111, 112
Kore, 4
Korokke, 84
Korosu, 118, 171
Kotsubo, 118
Kuma no kawa, 25
Kumo, 52
Kuradishonaru, 113–14
Kurisu, 66–67
Kuro, 100–101
Kurochū, 102
Kuro kutsu, 102
Kusa, 107
Kusachū, 108–9
Kuso, 21, 82, 161
Kusuri, 66
Kutsuname-ma, 20
Kyabasuke, 36, 37

181

Kyaku, 155
Kyakushitsunerai, 52
Kyandē, 43–44
Kyasshu, 46
Kyatchiman, 73
Kyokudo no kōfun, 130
Kyonchari, 27
Kyūjū, 164
Kyūkei, 43
Kyūri, 49
Kyūsho, 96–97

Mabuneta, 65
Machi no shirami, 22
Madamu kirā, 159
Mae o kasu, 32
Mageru, 172
Maki maki, 126
Maku, 108
Mambiki, 120
Mamosu gū, 54
Manējā, 72–73
Manko, 127
Manko yaru, 127
Manshon, 152–53
Manzuri, 103
Mappo, 34–35
Mara, 112, 126
Marifana, 101, 106–7
Marippana, 106–7
Marubi, 22
Marubo, 22
Masu, 38, 146
Masutabēshon, 38, 145–46
Matsu, 66
Matsutake, 49
Mechakucha gū, 54
Mechanko gū, 54
Megumi no ko, 31
Meiki, 71
Meiku, 36, 99, 114, 121
Mii-izumu, xii, 97

Mikuro seikatsu, 81
Mitsugu-kun, 76–77
Mō akimahen xvi
Mono, 6, 71
Mori mori, 164
Mosagamaru, 118
Moya moya no seki, 25–26
Muchi utsu, 39
Mune, 109
Musho, 92
Musuko, 38

Nako, 65
Naku, 131–32
Nama, 44, 101, 111–12
Namachū, 102
Namaensō, 112
Namajaku, 112
Nambā, xi
Nambaru, xv
Nambāyon, 65
Nampa, 16
Narichon, 27
Nau da, 54
Nauii, 54
Nekku, 113
Neko, 125, 140
Nekobaba, 120
Nekura, 113
Neko yaru, 125
Nenne, 140
Neru, 32, 46, 118, 129
Nesaseru, 172–73
Neta, 65
Netachi, 125
Nichi, 77–78
Nigiribobo, 104
Nigirippe, 62
Nikumanjū, 25–26
Ningen, 12
Ningyō, 104
Ninshin, 111, 112, 115–18

Nisegane, 48
Nisesatsu, 48
Nobi, 52
No-chichi, 18–19
Noguso, 163
Nokku, 117
Non-chichi, 18
Nonke, 46
Nōtarin, 9–10
Nozokibeya, 26
Nozoki-ma, 20
Nukani (san, yon, go, roku),
  132
Nusumu, 62, 119

Oban gyaru, 57
Obatarian, 100, 121, 159
Obatarian kirā, 159
Obu, 52
Ochinchin, 23–24
Ochoko, 71
Ōe, 14
Ofera, 43–44
Ofera kabuse, 44
Ofukuro gyaru, 57–58
Ogasumu, 130–31
Ohachi, 71
Ohayo, 52
Ohiki, 52
Oihagi, 154–55
Oinaribukuro, 97
Oinari-san, 97
Oisore, 56
Ojin gyaru, 58
Okama, 123–24, 138
Okama-chikku, 124
Okama-kusai, 124
Okama-ppoi, 124
Okama-rashii, 124
Okama-san, 123–24
Okanko, 129
Okeba, 99

Okera, 80
Okera onna, 80
Okera otoko, 80
Okkake, 52
Ōkii no, 164
Ōkii yatsu, 164–65
Ōkiku naru, 133
Omakosuri, 103–4
Omanko, 104, 126–29
Omankosuri, 103–4
Omeko, 104, 127–28
Omekosuri, 103–4
Onabe, 138
Onanii, 146
Onara, 8, 13, 63
Onē, 124
Onē-chan, 46
Onē-san, 124
Onkobo, 162–63
Onna no chikan, 20
Onnatarashi, 157–58
On za hiru, 110
Opampon, 23
Oppai, 109–10, 119
Ōrai, xvi
Ōrai geisha, xvi
Ōraru sekkusu, 44
Orugasumu, 130–31
Orugasumusu, 130
Osae, 53
Oshiiri, 53
Oshikko, 151
Oshikomi, 53
Oshiri, 93–95
Ososo, 128
Otachi, 139–40
Otankonasu, 10
Otenkinagashi, 53
Otokone, 30
Otoko-onna, 138
Ōtomachiku, 56
Otsutome, 92

Oyaji gyaru, 58
Ōzara, 70–71

Pachinko, 56
Paiotsu, 110
Paizuri, 110
Panku, 117
Pe, 65–66
Peboke, 67
Pēchan, 34
Pechapai, 110
Pechū, 67
Pekan, 67
Pe kutsu, 68
Penisu, 73
Penisu no shōnin, 73
Pēshan, 34
Pin, 133–35
Pinpin-chan, 134
Pinpon, 16
Pin to naru, 133–34
Pokochin, 23
Pombai, 75
Pombiki, 73
Pon, 75
Ponchū, 75
Ponkutsu, 75–76
Posuto, 154
Pōtā, 72–73
Potēto, 84
Potēto-chikku, 84–85

Rabā, 5, 5n
Ragiri, 126
Rakkyō, 49
Rakon, 30–31
Rāpon, 118
Rariru, 131
Retsuwaru, 93
Rezu, 137–38
Rezubian, 137–38
Rezu-kusa, 138

Rezu-kusai, 138
Rēzunpai, 110
Rezu-ppoi, 138
Rezuru, 138
Riki, 47
Risuku, 66
Rohe, 64
Ru, 47
Rumpen, 141
Ryōsei, 126
Ryōtōzukai, 125–26

Sabu, 12
Sachon, 27
Saikōchō, 130
Sairen, 116
Saka, 56
Sakachon, 27
Sakku, 44
Sane, 130
San esu zoku, 42
San nai gyaru, 58
Sannomu, 27
Sara, 70–71
Sarabobo, 128–29
Satsu, 91
Satsuma imo, 49
Sawari ma, 20
Sekkusu, 5, 8, 131, 132
Senzuri, 103, 145
Sewanuki, 53
Shaba, 92–93
Shaburu, 30
Shakuhachi, 112
Shatei, 12
Shigoki, 147
Shigoku, 147
Shigoto ni iku, 121
Shiiko, 151
Shiko, 151
Shiko shiko, 23, 146–47
Shimeru, 172

Shimo, 130
Shindarera furaito gyaru,
58
Shinjinai, xvii
Shippeta, 95
Shippiki, 56
Shirami, 22
Shiri, 93–95
Shiriba, 155–56
Shirigaru, 32
Shiri nuke, 11
Shiro, 66
Shiro-usagi, 53
Shishi, 151
Shōben, 149–50
Shombe, 151
Shomben, 149–51
Somunomu, 27
Sōnyū, 25, 69
Soso, 128–29
Sotoba, 155–56
Sugē gū, 54
Sugu hirogeru onna, 32
Suichi o ireru, 105
Sukashippe, 62
Suke, 15
Suki, 3
Sukkarakan, 81
Sukuri, 66
Sukuriin, xv
Suma no ura, 146
Sumara, 112
Sūpāeirian, xiv, 15
Sūpā etchi, 37
Supesharu sābisu, 112
Suri, 153
Suribachi, 71
Suriku, 66
Surippu, 112
Sutabēshon, 146
Sutan, xv
Sutorippā, 70, 95, 105, 126,

129, 135
Tachishomben, 149
Tachiyaku, 125, 139
Taima, 107
Taima Torishimari Hō, 107
Tai san, 108
Tama, 96
Tane, 65
Tanima no shirayuri, 110
Tarashi, 157
Tatamu, 172
Tatsu, 23, 30, 133
Tatta chimpo, 23
Tawake, 9
Tawakeru, 9
Te ga hayai, 157
Teikurō, 56
Temanko, 104
Temeko, 104
Tento o haru, 135
Tento mushi, 135n
Teppō mizu, 152–53
Teruho, 92
Tii-bii-esu, 14–15
Toguro, 164
Tokyo hōmuresu, 143
Tomaru, 116
Tomeru, 172
Torairin gyaru, 57
Torendii, xiii, 54–55
Tsugaru, 101–2
Tsukambe, 62–63
Tsukimakuru, 69, 70
Tsukkomu, 69, 71
Tsumannai, vii
Tsumannē, 114
Tsumu, 121–22
Tsūpin, 48
Tsura, 47
Tsureshōben, 149–50
Tsutsu, 152
Tsutsuharai, 152

185

Uchiba, 155–56
Uenomu, 27
Uguisu, 155
Uiri, 134
Uii-izumu, xii,97
Ukemi, 124–25
Ūman, xv
Unagi, 56
Unchi, 162
Unchingu sutairu, 162
Unko, 93, 161–62
Unko purē, 165
Unkozuwari, 160, 162
Ura, 47
Ura-omote, 125–26
Usunoro, 10
Utsu, 64–65, 74, 75
Utsuwa, 71

Warau, 121
Wareme-chan, 23
Watari, 47
Waibi, 155
Wakannai, xvii
Wanpatan, 167–68
Wappa hazushi, 154
Wayubi, 155

Yaburu, 93
Yaku, 153

Yamatesen, 147–48
Yande'ru, 114–15
Yāpi, 16
Yāpin, 101
Yari nashi, 79–80
Yaripon, 118
Yarisugi, 25
Yaru, 25, 32, 46, 94, 111, 112, 169–71
Yasagure, 142
Yasanuke, 141–42
Yojigen no shōnen, 25
Yōkei, 30–31
Yokochin moreru, 24
Yubi ningyō, 104–5
Yubitsukai, 148
Yubizeme, 104–5
Yūdachi, 152
Yuki, 66

Zaki, 98, 98n
Zakiru, 98, 98n
Zatōichi, 111–12
Zō chichi, 19, 34
Zoku, 11–12
Zumburi, 53
Zurakaru, 12, 22, 48, 167
Zurisen, 145

INDEX

AIDS, 44, 111–12
Ainu, 8n, 14, 106
Alcohol, mixing of, 17
Amphetamines, 74–76, 100, 107
Anal sex, 25, 94
Anus, 93–95, 104–5, 123
Approval, terms of, *vii*, 5, 53–55, 70, 72, 101, 120, 148
Argot. See *ingo*

Bachelor, 26–27
Beat up, 47, 119
Bisexual man, 125–26
Blackmailer, 29
Boring, 114, 167–69
Breaking wind, 12-13, 61–63
Breasts, 18–19, 109–10, 118
Burglar, 49–53, 119
Buttocks, 93–95

Chinese, *iv*, 3, 10, 87, 97, 101
Condom, 5n, 44, 111–12
Clitoris, 6, 105
Club-scene slang, 16, 35, 42, 53–54, 76–78, 113–15
Counterfeit money, 48

Depressed, 113-15
Destitute, 141–43
Dialects, *xvi–xvii*

Ashikaga, 10, 123n
Chiba, 93n
Chōzu, 160
Fukushima, *xvii*
Gifu, 93n
Hagagun, 123n,
Harima, 123, 150, 151
Hiroshima, 154
Hokuriku, 154
Ibaragi, 123
Jinji, 151
Kamitogagun, 123n
Kansai, *xvi*, 9, 69, 95
Kanuma, 10, 129
Kawachi-gun, 151
Kyoto, *xvi*, 154
Kyūshū 104, 128
Nagano, *xvii*
Nagasaki, *xv*
Nagoya, *xvii*, 9, 93n
Niigata, 93n
Osaka, *xvii*, 7, 8–9, 15, 24, 51, 61–62, 72, 81, 83, 89–90, 103–4, 105, 127–28, 154
Ōtawara, 11, 123n, 129
Oyama, 10, 52, 95, 129, 151
Sanno, 10, 123n, 129
Shikoku, 154
Shizuoka, *xvii*, 123n
Tochigi, 10, 52, 151
Tohoku, 62
Tokai, 15

Tokushima, 93n
Tokyo, *xvi, xix*, 93n
Toyama, 123
Utsunomiya, 10, 11, 130
Yaita, 129, 130
Yamagata, *xvii*
Yamanashi, *xvii*
Yokohama, *xvii*

Drinks, mixing of, 17
Drugs, 64–68, 74–76,
    100-102, 106–9, 153

Edo period, *iii*, 79, 87–88,
    89, 97, 101
Ejaculation, 32–33, 41, 111,
    132
Enema, 20, 165. *See also*
    Perversion
Erection, *xv*, 6, 30, 133–35
Escape, 12, 22, 40, 48, 93,
    167
Expletives:
    Aa, 61, 85, 96, 103, 116,
        126, 138, 139, 151, 161–62
    Ara, 31
    Baka, 21
    Baka yarō, 91
    Bukimi, 135
    Chikushō, 21, 32, 116
    Gee, 83, 96
    Kuso, 21, 163
    Masaka, 77
    Mō, 61, 85, 151
    Na, 68, 128, 165
    Ne (nē), 4, 5, 41, 68, 77,
        103, 107, 116, 124, 125,
        146, 158
    Oē, 14
    Oi, 6, 19, 65, 75, 84, 107
    Omae, 37
    Omē, 12, 104, 107, 149

Omē yo, 120
Saitei, 33
Shinjirarenai, 121
Shinjirarenē, 96, 120, 139
Sugē, 70
Sugoi ze, 101
Torendii jan, vii
Yaru jan, 5, 72
Yatta, 148

Feces, 21, 82, 93, 149,
    161–65
Fellatio, 30, 43–4, 112
Foreigner, derogatory
    terms for, 31, 35, 99

Gaudiness, 35–36, 97–100
German, 40, 130, 141, 146
Glans, 23. *See also* Penis
Gun, 55–56

Haiku, 61n, 151n
Heian period, 7, 123
Hermaphrodite, 126
Heroin, 64-68
Homosexual, 45–46, 116
    123–26, 137–40
Hoodlum, 11-12, 21, 29–30
Hymen, *xv*

Idiot, 7–11, 27, 62
Ingo (secret criminal
    language) *xiii*, 46–48,
    49–53, 55–56, 79–80, 93,
    98, 110, 118, 121–22, 135,
    141–43,153–56, 171–73
Irresponsibility, 17–18

Kill, 47, 118, 119, 171–73
Knife, 55–56
Korean, 3, 26–27

Lesbian, 42, 116, 137–40
Love, 3–5
Lover, 4–5
  female, 15, 55, 126, 140
  male, 16, 38, 39, 72,
    76–78, 81, 105

Makeup, 35–36, 99, 114,
  121
Marijuana, 101, 106–9
Masseuse, 104, 110
Masturbation, 23, 30, 38
  female, 103–6
  in public, 148
  male, 145–48
  using breasts, 110
Me-ism, *xii*, 97
Meiji period, *xv, xvi*, 47,
  130, 137
Men: attractive, 157
  derogatory terms for, 27,
    58–59, 83–85, 89, 99,
    157–59, 172
  unattractive, 14-15
Money, 29, 46–48, 73, 122,
  156, 172
Motorcycle gang. *See*
  Hoodlums

Negativity, 113–15
No, 15–16
Not up to par, 82–83

Obesity, 33-34, 114, 117,
  124
Opium, 100–102
Orgasm, 32–33, 130–32

Peepshow, 26
Penetration, 25, 68–70
Penis, 20, 22, 23–24, 30–31
  38, 49, 71, 96, 110, 126,

  129n, 131, 133–35, 146,
    152
  circumcized, 30–31, 49
  derogatory term for, 146
  erect, 133-35
  exposure of, 24
  large, 24
  small, 31
Perversion, 37–38, 148, 165
Pervert, 19–20
Pickpocket, 46, 153–56
Pimp, 29, 71–73, 115
Playboy, 157–59
Police, 27, 34–35, 91, 172
Pornography, 39–40
Poverty, 79–82
Pregnancy, 111, 112,
  115–18
Prison, 22, 90–93, 173
Prostitute, 36, 87–88
Proverbs, 49n, 63, 87–88,
  94–95, 97, 149–50
Provincial person, 83–85

Robber, 49–53, 119
Roman alphabet, *xv*, 5, 9,
  14, 37–39, 40–42, 65–66

Sadomasochism, 20, 39,
  46, 95
Sanskrit, 7n, 55, 92
Sex, *xv*, 5, 8, 16, 24–25, 32,
  38, 41, 46, 94, 98n, 111–
  12, 117, 118, 125, 129n,
  131, 132
Smoking, 41
Soapland massage parlor,
  iii, 104–05, 110–12, 131,
  148
Sperm, 41, 110
Squat, 162
Stingy, 89–90

Stripper, 70, 95, 105, 126, 129, 135

Teenage slang, *xvi*, 5, 9, 14–15, 18–19, 25, 35–36, 40–42, 81–83, 84–85, 108, 110, 113–15, 116, 124, 134, 147–48, 151–52, 157–59, 162, 167–69
Testicles, 6, 95–97
Theft, 49, 119–22
Thief's tools, 55–56

Ugliness, *xiv*, 14–15, 114
Urination, 149–53

Vagina, 6, 23, 25–26, 70–71, 103–5, 123n, 126–30, 140, 152

Vibrator, 68, 104
Virgin, 37, 71
Vomit, 14, 83
Voyeur, 20

We-ism, *xii*, 97
Women, *xv*, *xvi*, 20, 26, 57–59
   attractive, 19
   derogatory terms for, 14–15, 31–32, 36, 37, 42, 99–100, 114, 116, 121, 137–40, 172
   pickpockets, 154

Yakuza, 21–22, 26–27, 34–35, 46–48, 75, 92, 100, 115, 171
Yes, 16